M000042746

ANOTHER BEAUTY

ANOTHER BEAUTY

ADAM ZAGAJEWSKI

TRANSLATED FROM THE POLISH BY

CLARE CAVANAGH

FOREWORD BY SUSAN SONTAG

THE UNIVERSITY OF GEORGIA PRESS

ATHENS

Published in 2002 by the University of Georgia Press
Athens, Georgia 30602
www.ugapress.org
© 2000 by Adam Zagajewski
Translation © 2000 by Clare Cavanagh
Foreword © 2001 by Susan Sontag
All rights reserved
Published by arrangement with
Farrar, Straus and Giroux, LLC

Printed digitally in the United States of America

Library of Congress Cataloging-in-Publication Data

Zagajewski, Adam, 1945–
[W cudzym pieknie. English]
Another beauty / Adam Zagajewski ; translated from the
Polish by Clare Cavanagh ; foreword by Susan Sontag.
xxiii, 215 p. ; 21 cm.
ISBN 0-8203-2410-8 (pbk. : alk. paper)
I. Cavanagh, Clare. II. Title.
PG7185.A32 W213 2002
791.8'587303—dc21
[B]   2001052262

ISBN-13: 978-0-8203-2410-4

Originally published in 1998 by
Wydawnictwo a5, Poland, as *W cudzym pieknie*

First published in the United States by
Farrar, Straus and Giroux in 2000

ANOTHER BEAUTY
(from *Tremor*)

We find comfort only in
another beauty, in others'
music, in the poetry of others.
Salvation lies with others,
though solitude may taste like
opium. Other people aren't hell
if you glimpse them at dawn, when
their brows are clean, rinsed by dreams.
This is why I pause: which word
to use, you or he. Each he
betrays some you, but
calm conversation bides its time
in others' poems.

—translated by Clare Cavanagh

THE WISDOM PROJECT

Susan Sontag

Another Beauty, a wise, iridescent book by the Polish writer Adam Zagajewski, dips in and out of many genres: coming-of-age-memoir, commonplace book, aphoristic musings, vignettes, and defense of poetry—that is, a defense of the idea of literary greatness.

It is, to be sure, something of a misnomer to call Zagajewski a writer: a poet who also writes indispensable prose does not thereby forfeit the better title. Prose being the wordy affair it is, Zagajewski's fills a good many more pages than his poems. But in literature's canonical two-party system, poetry always trumps prose. Poetry stands for literature at its most serious, most improving, most intense, most coveted. "The author and reader always dream of a great poem, of writing it, reading it, living it." Living the poem: being elevated by it; deepened; for a moment, saved.

From a great Polish writer we expect Slavic intensities. (The particular Polish nuance may require a little application.) Literature as soul nourishment has been a Slavic specialty for the last century and a half. It seems hardly surprising that Zagajewski, for all the calm and delicacy of his poet-voice, would hold a view of poetry more akin to that of Shelley than of Ashbery. As it happens, the reality of self-transcendence has even less credibility among younger Polish poets than among those writing in English. And Zagajewski's transposed religious longings—to live, through poetry, on a "higher plane"—are never voiced without a grace note of mild

self-deprecation. A recent collection of poems is called, with charming sobriety, *Mysticism for Beginners*. The world (of lyrical feeling,
of ecstatic inwardness) to which poetry gives poets and their readers access is one that defective human nature bars us from inhabit-
ing except fleetingly. Poems "don't last," Zagajewski observes wryly,
"particularly the short lyric poems that prevail today." All they can
offer is "a moment of intense experience." Prose is sturdier, if only
because it takes longer to get through.

Another Beauty is Zagajewski's third book of prose to appear in
English. The first two are made up of pieces, some essayistic, some
memoiristic, with titles. The new book is a flow of untitled (and
unnumbered) short and not so short takes, as brief as a sentence, as
long as several pages. Its mix of narratives, observations, portraits,
reflections, reminiscences gives *Another Beauty* a high-velocity vari-
ance of mood and attack that we associate more with a volume of
poems—lyric poems, anyway—which is a succession of discontinuous intensities, at different pitches of concern.

What kind of intensities? (That is, what kind of prose?)
Thoughtful, precise; rhapsodic; rueful; courteous; prone to wonder. Then and now, here and there—the whole book oscillates,
vibrates, with contrasts. (This is like this, but that is like that. Or:
we expected this, but we got that.) And everything reeks of dissimi-
larity, savor, message, metaphor. Even the weather:

> The meteorological depressions of Paris have an oceanic feel;
> the Atlantic dispatches them in the direction of the continent. The
> winds blow, dark clouds scurry across the city like racecars. The
> rain falls at a spiteful slant. At times the heavens' face appears,
> a scrap of blue. Then it's dark again, the Seine becomes a black
> pavement. The lowlands of Paris seethe with oceanic energy, thun-
> derbolts pop like champagne corks. Whereas a typical Central Eu-
> ropean depression—centered somewhere above the Carpathians—
> behaves completely differently: it's subdued and melancholy, one

might say philosophical. The clouds barely move. They're shaped differently; they're like an enormous blimp drooping over Kraków's Central Market. The light shifts gradually; the violet glow fades, giving way to yellow spotlights. The sun skulks somewhere behind silken clouds, illuminating the most varied strata of earth and sky. Some of the clouds resemble deep-sea fishes that have ascended to the surface and swim with mouths wide open, as if startled by the taste of air. This kind of weather can last for several days, the meek climate of Central Europe. And if, after lengthy deliberations, a thunderstorm does strike, it behaves as if it were stuttering. Instead of a sharp, decisive shot, it emits a series of drawn-out sounds, *pa pa pa pa*—an echo instead of a blast. Thunder on the installment plan.

In Zagajewski's rendering, nature turns out to be wittily steeped in the bathos of national histories, with the crisp, bullying weather of Paris flaunting France's indefatigable good fortune and Kraków's tired, melancholy weather summing up Poland's innumerable defeats and other woes. The poet can't escape history, only transmute it sometimes, for purposes of bravura descriptiveness, into magic geography.

May you be born in interesting times, runs the ancient (or at least proverbial) Chinese curse. Updated for our hyperinteresting era, it might run: May you be born in an interesting place.

What Czeslaw Milosz calls, mordantly, "the privilege of coming from strange lands where it is difficult to escape history"—think of Poland, Ireland, Israel, Bosnia—prods and pinches, exalts and exhausts a writer like Zagajewski whose standards are set by *world* literature. History means strife. History means tragic impasse—and your friends being jailed or killed. History means perennial challenges to the nation's very right to exist. Poland, of course, had two centuries of history's chokehold—from the First Partition in 1772, which in a few years brought about the end of an autonomous state (not restored until after World War I) to the collapse of the Soviet-style regime in 1989.

Such countries—such histories—make it hard for their writers ever completely to secede from the collective anguish. Here is the testimony of another great writer living in a newer nation condemned to nonstop dread, A. B. Yehoshua:

> You are insistently summoned to solidarity, summoned from within yourself rather than by an external compulsion, because you live from one newscast to the next, and it becomes a solidarity that is technical, automatic from the standpoint of its emotional reaction, because by now you are completely built to react that way and live in tension. Your emotional reactions to any piece of news about an Israeli casualty, a plane shot down, are predetermined. Hence the lack of solitude, the inability to be alone in the spiritual sense and to arrive at a life of intellectual creativity.

Yehoshua's terms are identical with those of Zagajewski, whose first prose book in English is a collection of six pieces published in the early 1980s called *Solidarity, Solitude*. Solitude erodes solidarity; solidarity corrupts solitude.

The solitude of a Polish writer is always inflected by a sense of the community formed by the literature itself. Milosz, in his own great defense of poetry, the address that he delivered at the Jagiellonian University in 1989 entitled "With Polish Poetry against the World," pays homage to Polish poetry for having protected him "from sterile despair in emigration," recalling that "in solitude too difficult and painful to recommend to anyone" there was always "the sense of duty toward my predecessors and successors." For Milosz, born in 1911, a Polish writer may never escape being responsible to others. By this rule, the stellar counterexample of Witold Gombrowicz—in his fiction, in his legendarily egocentric, truculent *Diary*, in his brazen polemic "Against Poetry"—offers evidence,

convulsive evidence, of the authority of idealism in Polish literature. History is present, even by its absence, Milosz observes in a
late book of prose, *Milosz's ABC*; and the cult of altruism and high-
mindedness flourishes, if perversely, in Gombrowicz's denial of
responsibility to anything beyond the self's anarchic clamor, his
ingenious harangues on behalf of the menial, the immature, the low-
minded.

Squeezed right, every life can be construed as embodying exemplary experiences and historical momentousness. Even
Gombrowicz could not help but see his life as exemplary, making
something didactic—a rebuke to his origins—out of his gentry
childhood, his precocious literary notoriety, his fateful, irrevocable
emigration. And a writer whose love of literature still entailed,
unresentfully, so much piety toward old masters, such eagerness to
feed on the magnificent traditions on offer from the past, could
hardly help seeing his life—at least his early circumstances—as some
kind of representative destiny.

Soon after Zagajewski's birth in October 1945 in the mediaeval
Polish city of Lwów, his family was uprooted in the great displacements (and redrawings of maps) that followed the Yalta agreements
of the Three Old Men, which put Lwów in the hands of the Soviet
Union; and the poet grew up in the formerly German, now Polish,
town of Gliwice, thirty miles from Auschwitz. In *Two Cities*, his
second prose book translated into English, Zagajewski writes:

> I spent my childhood in an ugly industrial city; I was brought there
> when I was barely four months old, and then for many years after-
> ward I was told about the extraordinarily beautiful city that my
> family had to leave.

The family mythology of an expulsion from paradise may have
made him feel, he says, forever homeless. It also seems, on the evidence of his writing, to have made him an expert lover of cities—
"beautiful, bewitching Kraków," above all, for which he left unre-

deemable Gliwice to attend university, and where he remained until he was thirty-seven.

Dates are sparse in *Another Beauty*, and the arrangement of stories-from-a-life is unchronological. But there is, implicitly, always a *where*, with which the poet's heart and senses are in dialogue. Not the traveler, not even the émigré—most of the great Polish poets have gone westward, and Zagajewski is not one of the exceptions—but the continually stimulated city-dweller is featured here. There are few living rooms and no bedrooms in *Another Beauty*, but more than a few public squares and libraries and trains. Once he is past his student years, the occasional "we" disappears; there is only an "I." Occasionally he will mention where he is writing: Zagajewski now lives in Paris and teaches one term each year at the University of Houston. "I'm strolling through Paris," one entry begins. "And at this very moment I'm listening to the Seventh Symphony in Houston," notes another. There are always two cities: Lwów and Gliwice, Gliwice and Kraków, Paris and Houston.

More poignant oppositions infuse this book: self and others, youth and age. There are plangent evocations of difficult elderly relatives and cranky professors: this portrait of the poet as a young man is striking for its tenderness toward the old. And the account of the decorous ardors, literary and political, of his student years sets his book quite at odds with the narcissistic purposes, and pointedly indiscreet contents, of most autobiographical writing today. For Zagajewski, autobiography is an occasion to purge oneself of vanity, while advancing the project of self-understanding—call it the wisdom project—which is never completed, however long the life.

To describe oneself as young is to face that one is no longer young. And a pithy acknowledgment that the debilities of age approach, with death in their train, is one of the many observations that cut short a story from Zagajewski's past. Telling the stories discontinuously, as glimpses, secures several good results. It keeps the prose dense, quick. And it invites telling only those stories that lead to some insight, or epiphany. There is a larger lesson in the very way of telling, a lesson in moral tone: how to talk about one-self without complacency. Life, when not a school for heartlessness, is an education in sympathy. The sum of the stories reminds us that in a life of a certain length and spiritual seriousness, change—some-times not for the worse—is just as real as death.

All writing is a species of remembering. If there is anything triumphalist about *Another Beauty* it is that the acts of remember-ing the book contains seem so frictionless. Imagining—that is, bringing the past to mental life—is there as needed; it never fal-ters; it is by definition a success. The recovery of memory, of course, is an ethical obligation: the obligation to persist in the effort to apprehend the truth. This seems less apparent in America, where the work of memory has been exuberantly identified with the cre-ation of useful or therapeutic fictions, than in Zagajewski's lacer-ated corner of the world.

To recover a memory—to secure a truth—is a supreme touch-stone of value in *Another Beauty*. "I didn't witness the extermina-tion of the Jews," he writes:

> I was born too late. I bore witness, though, to the gradual process by which Europe recovered its memory. This memory moved slowly, more like a lazy, lowland river than a mountain stream, but it finally, unambiguously condemned the evil of the Holocaust and the Nazis, and the evil of Soviet civilization as well (though in this it was less successful, as if reluctant to admit that two such mon-strosities might simultaneously coexist).

That memories are recovered—that is, that the suppressed truths do reemerge—is the basis of whatever hope one can have for jus-tice and a modicum of sanity in the ongoing life of communities. Once recovered, though, even truth may become complacent

and self-flattering. Thus, rather than provide yet one more denun-
ciation of the iniquities and oppressiveness of the regime that was
shut down in 1989, Zagajewski chooses to stress the benefits of the
struggle against evil that flowed to the idealistic young in his por-
trayal of the flawed beginnings of his vocation, as a "political poet,"
and his activities in dissident student and literary circles in the
Kraków of the late 1960s and 1970s. (In 1968, Zagajewski was
twenty-three years old.) In those heady days, poetry and activism
rhymed. Both elevated, heightened; engagement in a just cause, like
service to poetry, made you feel larger.

   That every generation fears, misunderstands, and condescends
to its successor—this, too, is a function of the equivalence of
history and memory (history being what it is agreed on, collectively,
to remember). Each generation has its distinctive memories,
and the elapsing of time, which brings with it a steady accumulation of loss, confers on those memories a normativeness which
cannot possibly be honored by the young, who are busy compiling
their memories, their benchmarks. One of Zagajewski's most moving portraits of elders is of Stefan Szuman, an illustrious member
of the interwar Polish intelligentsia (he had known Stanislaw
Witkiewicz and Bruno Schulz) and now a retired professor at
the university living in isolation and penury. Its point is Zagajewski's
realization, thinking back, that he and his literary friends could
only have seemed like fools and savages, "shaped by a postwar education, by new schools, new papers, new radio, new TV," to the
defeated, homely, embittered Szuman and his wife. The rule seems
to be: each generation looks upon its successor generation as
barbarians.

   Zagajewski, himself no longer young and now a teacher of
American students, is committed to not replicating, in his turn, that
kind of despair and incomprehension. Nor is he content to write
off an entire older Polish generation of intellectuals and artists, his
generation's "enemy"—the true believers and those who just sold

out—for turpitude and cowardice: they weren't simply devils, any more than he and his friends were angels. As for those "who began by serving Stalin's civilization" but then changed, Zagajewski writes: "I don't condemn them for their early, youthful intoxication. I'm more inclined to marvel at the generosity of human nature, which offers gifted young people a second chance, the opportunity for a moral comeback."

At the heart of this assessment is the wisdom of the novelist, a professional of empathy, rather than that of a lyric poet. (Zagajewski has written four novels, none as yet translated into English.) The dramatic monologue "Betrayal" in *Two Cities* begins:

> Why did I do that? Why did I do what? Why was I who I was? And who was I? I am already beginning to regret that I agreed to grant you this interview. For years I refused; you must have asked me at a weak moment or in a moment of anxiety. . . . What did that world look like? The one you were too late to get to know. The same as this one. Completely different.

That everything is always different . . . and the same: a poet's wisdom. Actually, wisdom *tout court*.

Of course, history should never be thought of with a capital H. The governing sense of Zagajewski's memory-work is his awareness of having lived through several historical periods, in the course of which things eventually got better. Modestly, imperfectly—not utopianly—better. The young Zagajewski and his comrades in dissidence had assumed that communism would last another hundred, two hundred years, when, in fact, it had less than two decades to go. Lesson: evil is not immutable. The reality is, everyone outlives an old self, often more than one, in the course of a reasonably long life.

Another Beauty is, in part, a meditation on easing the clamp of history: liberating the self from "the grimaces and caprices" of history. That should not be so hard in the less flagrantly evil public world that has come into being in Poland since 1989. But institutions may be more easily liquidated than a temperament. Zagajewski's temperament (that is, the dialogue he conducts with himself) is rooted in an era where heroism was at least an option, and ethical rigor still something admired and consecrated by the genius of several national literatures. How to negotiate a soft landing onto the new lowland of diminished moral expectations and shabby artistic standards is the problem of all the Central European writers whose tenacities were forged in the bad old days.

The maturing that Zagajewski chronicles can be described as the relaxing of this temperament: the finding of the right openness, the right calmness, the right inwardness. (He says he can only write when he feels happy, peaceful.) Exaltation—and who can gainsay this judgment from a member of the generation of '68?—is viewed with a sceptical eye. Hyperemphatic intensity holds no allure. His end of the religious spectrum does not include any notion of the sacred, which figures centrally in the work of the late Jerzy Grotowski and the theatre center in Gardzienice led by Wlodzimierz Staniewski. While the sacral-ecstatic tradition is still alive in Polish theatre—but then theatre, especially this kind of theatre, is compulsorily collective—it has no place in contemporary Polish literature. *Another Beauty* is suffused with the humility of a spiritual longing that precludes frenzy, and envisages no large gestures of sacrifice. As Zagajewski notes: "The week isn't made up only of Sundays."

Some of his keenest pages are descriptions of happiness, the everyday happiness of a connoisseur of solitary delights: strolling, reading, listening to Beethoven or Schumann. The "I" of *Another Beauty* is scrupulous, vulnerable, earnest—without a jot of self-protective irony. And neither Zagajewski nor this reader would wish it otherwise. Irony would come at the cost of so much pleasure. "Ecstasy and irony rarely meet in the world of art," Zagajewski observes. "When they do it's usually for the purposes of mutual sabotage; they struggle to diminish each other's power." And he is unabashedly on the side of ecstasy.

These descriptions are tributes to what produces happiness, not celebrations of the receptive self. He may simply describe something he loves, or quote a favorite poem: the book is a sampling of appreciations and sympathies. There are penetrating sketches of admired friends such as Adam Michnik, a beacon of resistance to the dictatorship (who while in jail wrote about the poet Zbigniew Herbert, among others, in a book he titled *From the History of Honor in Poland*); there is a reverential salute to the ancient doyen of Polish émigrés in Paris, the painter, writer, and heroic alumnus of Soviet prison camps, Jozef Czapski. *L'enfer, c'est les autres*. No, it is others who save us, Zagajewski declares in the poem that gives the book its title and serves as its epigraph.

Here is "Another Beauty" in the new version by the book's translator, Clare Cavanagh.

> We find comfort only in
> another beauty, in others'
> music, in the poetry of others.
> Salvation lies with others,
> though solitude may taste like
> opium. Other people aren't hell
> if you glimpse them at dawn, when
> their brows are clean, rinsed by dreams.
> This is why I pause: which word
> to use, you or he. Each he
> betrays some you, but
> calm conversation bides its time
> in others' poems.

And here it is as it appeared in 1985 in *Tremor: Selected Poems*, Zagajewski's first collection of poems in English, translated by

Renata Gorczynski, where it is entitled "In the Beauty Created by Others":

Only in the beauty created
by others is there consolation,
in the music of others and in others' poems.
Only others save us,
even though solitude tastes like
opium. The others are not hell,
if you see them early, with their
foreheads pure, cleansed by dreams.
That is why I wonder what
word should be used, "he" or "you." Every "he"
is a betrayal of a certain "you" but
in return someone else's poem
offers the fidelity of a sober dialogue.

A defense of poetry *and* a defense of goodness, or, more exactly, of good-naturedness.

Nothing could take the reader in a more contrary direction to today's cult of the excitements of self than to follow Zagajewski as he unspools his seductive praise of serenity, sympathy, forbearance; of "the calm and courage of an ordinary life." To declare "I believe in truth!" and, in another passage, "Goodness does exist!" (those exclamation points!) seems, if not Panglossian—one American reviewer detected a touch of Panglossian uplift in the book—then at least quixotic. This culture offers few current models of masculine sweetness, and those we already possess, from past literature, are associated with naïveté, childlikeness, social innocence: Joe Gargery in *Great Expectations*, Alyosha in *The Brothers Karamazov*. Zagajewski's persona in *Another Beauty* is anything but innocent in that sense. But he has a special gift for conjuring up states of complex innocence, the innocence of genius, as in his heartrending portrait-poem "Franz Schubert: A Press Conference."

The title may mislead. *Another Beauty* makes clear at every turn that, worshipper of greatness in poetry and other arts that he is, Zagajewski is not an aesthete. Poetry is to be judged by standards still higher: "Woe to the writer who values beauty over truth." Poetry must be protected from the temptations to arrogance inherent in its own states of elation.

Of course, both beauty and truth seem like frail guideposts left over from a more innocent past. In the delicate negotiation with the present that Zagajewski conducts on behalf of the endangered verities, nostalgia would count as a deficit of argument. Still, even absent the old certainties and license to perorate, he is pledged to defending the idea of "sublime" or "noble" achievement in literature—assuming, as he does, that we still need the qualities in art that are praised by such now virtually unsayable words. Zagajewski's most eloquent, summative defense is "The Shabby and the Sublime," an address he delivered at a Dutch university in 1998, which posed the pseudo-naïve question: is literary greatness still possible?

The belief in literary greatness implies that the capacity for admiration is still intact. When admiration is corrupted, that is, made cynical, the question as to whether greatness is possible simply vanishes. Nihilism and admiration compete with each other, sabotage each other, struggle to diminish each other's power. (Like irony and ecstasy.)

Disheartened though he is by "the mutation downward of European literature," Zagajewski declines to speculate about what has given the advantage to subjectivism and the revolt against "greatness." Perhaps those brought up on the fierceness of state-administered mediocrity find it hard to be as indignant as they might be about the extent to which mercantilist values (often sporting the

mask of "democratic" or populist values) have sapped the foundations of the sublime. "Soviet civilization," a.k.a. communism, was
a great conservative force. The cultural policies of communist re-
gimes embalmed the old, hierarchical notions of achievement, seeking to confer a noble pedigree on propagandistic banalities. In contrast, capitalism has a truly radical relation to culture, dismantling
the very notion of greatness in the arts, which is now most successfully dismissed by the ecumenical philistinism of both cultural
progressives and cultural reactionaries as an "elitist" presumption.

Zagajewski's protest against the collapse of standards has nothing analytical about it. Yet surely he understands the futility (and
indignity) of simply denouncing the collapse. Orphaned pieties
overheat sometimes: "Without poetry, we'd hardly be better than
the mammals." And many passages assert a familiar dismay, especially when he succumbs to the temptation to see our era as uniquely
degraded. What, he inquires rhetorically, would "the great, innocent artists of the past, Giotto or van Eyck, Proust or Apollinaire,
have done if some spiteful demon had set them down in our flawed
and tawdry world?" Don't know about Giotto or van Eyck; but
Proust (d. 1924) and Apollinaire (d. 1918) *innocent?* I should have
thought the Europe in which that colossal, senseless slaughter called
World War I took place was, if anything, a good deal worse than
"flawed and tawdry."

The idea of art as the beleaguered vehicle of spiritual value in a
secular age should not have been left unexamined. Nevertheless,
Zagajewski's utter absence of rancor and vindictiveness, his generosity of spirit, his awareness of the vulgarity of unremitting com-
plaint and of the self-righteous assumption of one's own cultural
superiority, mark off his stance from that of the usual tribe of professional mourners of the Death of High Culture, such as the ever
portentous George Steiner. (Once in a while he slips into facile
assertions about the superiority of the past over the present,

but even then he is never grandiose or self-aggrandizing: call it Steinerism with a human face.)

Inveterately prescriptive, occasionally sententious, Zagajewski is too shrewd, too respectful of common or ordinary wisdom, not to see the limits of each of the positions that surround and make sense out of his abiding passions. One *can* be elevated, deepened, improved by works of art. But, Zagajewski cautions, the imagination can become one of its own enemies "if it loses sight of the solid world that cannot be dissolved in art."

Because the book is notational, juxtapositional, it is possible for Zagajewski to entertain quite contradictory assessments. What is valuable is how divided Zagajewski is, as he himself acknowledges. The reflections and the stories in *Another Beauty* show us a subtle, important mind divided between the public world and the claims of art, between solidarity and solitude; between the original "two cities": the Human City and the City of God. Divided, but not overthrown. There is anguish, but then serenity keeps breaking through. There is desolation and, as well, so many fortifying pleasures supplied by the genius of others. There was scorn, until *caritas* chimed in. There is despair, but there is, just as inexorably, consolation.

ANOTHER BEAUTY

Dluga Street didn't belong to our world. It had little in common with the historical moment, with the moment designated by that proud, often misused phrase "the present day." It was a flagrant anachronism, even though a few steps away Warsaw Street ran obligingly in the direction of the capital and Dluga Street itself bisected Three Poets' Boulevard, already a busy thoroughfare by the 1960s. But of course this kind of distance from the reigning age is something completely different for a street than it is for living, feeling people. Streets are usually mindless: their low brows don't conceal hope, despair, or ideas. The rooftops rest placidly on apartment buildings. But one may suppose or suspect certain things nonetheless. Thus it seems to me that Dluga Street preferred horses and horse-drawn carriages. Peasant carts probably suited it best, but it had no objection to smart coaches with cushioned rubber wheels rolling merrily on their springs. There was a place for such things, they fit the street's tricky character. In the winter fragrant horse dung garnished the white snow with yellow spots, steaming lavishly; it lured the local sparrows, greedy for any sort of diversion. Dluga Street was caught painfully off guard by modern history. It didn't like electricity or internal combustion engines; it didn't like Hitlerism, introduced by the triumphant Wehrmacht, or Stalinism, imported by the Red Army. It would have been happy with horses, carts, and the sweet scent of manure. Servants'

shouting, the parasols of elegant ladies, the changing seasons, rain,
snow, and sun—these would have filled its modest life completely.
Some of these enduring things lingered on. In the fall, heaps of coal
rose on the sidewalk, transported in scuttles, or shoveled with
spades straight into cellars. Before the Christmas holidays, firs and
pines sprouted on balconies, and luckless, bug-eyed carps with
voluptuous lips were brought home by patresfamilias in nets from
which drops of water fled. There, in the dense hedgerows of apartment houses rubbing walls in solidarity as if boosting one another's
spirits in troubled times, there on the fourth floor, lay the tiny
estate of Mrs. C., where I rented my first room in Krakow.

Mrs. C. is doubtless no longer living. Mrs. C. would certainly
not have wanted her noble surname disclosed to the reading public.
Thus she will remain simply Mrs. C., former member of the landed
gentry—an F.L.G., FLAG, as they were usually known—although
now, after the war, she governed not an entire estate but a single
small apartment.

I didn't know much about her. I didn't know what had happened
to her husband, or if she'd actually ever been married. I didn't know
if she had children, and if so, where they lived. Mrs. C. despised her
tenants and almost never spoke with them, that is, with us. Her personal life, the prehistory of her present existence, thus could not be
uncovered. But no, I misspoke, she didn't despise her tenants, it
wasn't anything so simple, so vulgar. Her true residence was elsewhere, in a different realm, in some imperceptible, inscrutable reg-
ister of the cosmos. She wasn't there among us, among those who
had agreed that the gray world of Communism actually did exist.
She refused to endorse a treaty with Reality; she performed in a different theater, dwelled in a different country. She wasn't among
us—we met her only in the apartment's corridor, a dismal hallway
that called to mind the ruined parts of town. Mrs. C. was determined to maintain her prewar status in this shabby setting. She had
decided to remain an heiress, the mistress of an estate, and contin-

ued to look down her nose at those from other walks of life. This
decision determined everything, since she wasn't actually distinguished in any way, she didn't know any more than ordinary people,
she wasn't a blue blood, a true aristocrat. She was a short, heavy
woman with a cross, homely face like a crushed doughnut, hair of
an indeterminate color, and a damp, unpleasant voice.

Her policy was simply not to appear, to leave the parlor that was
also her bedroom as seldom as possible. To be invisible, not to be
swallowed up in others' eyes, to shield her essence—but what was
her essence?—from contact with other essences. She almost never
left the house, and exhaustive preparations preceded her infrequent
outings, as if major international publications had sent swarms of
photojournalists to lie in wait for her on the street. Once I heard
her say, "Each exit is my Rapallo." Why Rapallo? She probably
didn't know herself, but Rapallo had a nice, round ring to it. From
time to time she entertained company—aging ladies drawn only
from her own class, the F.L.G.'s—and then only in the afternoon, at
English teatime, never for dinner in the evening.

Mrs. C. was preoccupied with her historical mission, with the
defense of her own social position, the defense of feudalism in a
hostile Communist environment. It was taboo to touch a broom,
peel potatoes, wash the floor, make dinner. Such seemingly incon-
sequential actions could lead to only one thing: the annihilation of
her higher substance, the substance that was her greatest and—why
beat around the bush?—only treasure. If she were to make herself a
soft-boiled egg or fry a schnitzel, then the dignity of an entire era
would collapse with a crash, the Middle Ages would finally grind to
a halt.

Fortunately, there was someone to wash the windows and
floors, do the shopping, make lunch and dinner: Helena, the maid,
the servant, the serf. Helena got up every day at 4 a.m. and took the
early streetcar—full of desperadoes with eyes red from exhaus-
tion—in to work. She worked as a janitor in the city's center for rat

control and perhaps as a result she herself looked a little like a rat: she had a narrow snout, a straight nose, and small, bright eyes. She was short and deft, restless and meddlesome. No one ever did battle for this Helen beneath the walls of Troy. When she left for work at dawn, the rest of the apartment house had not yet woken up; most of the town's inhabitants were still sound asleep. Mrs. C. was undoubtedly asleep, I was sleeping, and so was my roommate, an enigmatic engineering student two years older than myself. The entire house woke up only around seven-thirty when Helena returned with the brisk air of one who had done her small part in exterminating the city's vermin. Helena came home from work just as bleary civil servants were approaching the city's many office buildings, and as the rats lay down to sleep in their lairs.

Helena was called upon to deal with the outside world, with history and nature, with pigeons and crows, with cats, with the milkman, mailman, and chimney sweep, with soot and milk. She was the one who handled concrete objects; she inhaled dust, polished the doorknobs, and scoured the kettle. She was always in a rush, no time to rest, she hurried and scurried. She slept in the kitchen, on a couch covered with a brown bedspread by day. At night she pored over the local paper by lamplight; this was her only chance to contemplate the varieties of human folly. She would put on her wire-rimmed glasses and scrutinize the events listed in the crime column: someone had murdered someone else, out of love or envy, for money. I think she sighed then with relief, since this meant the world had not entirely lost its earlier, prewar imagination and wasn't yet reduced to meetings of the one party's central committee. Mrs. C. handed down instructions, managed the expenses, and, like any minister of finance, complained about costs and Helena's unconscionable overspending.

From time to time horrific quarrels erupted between the mistress and her galley slave for no apparent reason; as in an arsenal, the slightest spark could set off an explosion. Helena would give her oppressor notice, slam the door, run out of the house, come back, slam the door again, and scream, "I've had it! Why is it always me, me, me, always just me." Because of her daily streetcar rides and her contact with people, Helena had a better grasp of what was actually happening in Krakow and the country. She was the one who sensed the city's shifting moods; she was the one who read the paper, even though she only read the crime column. In theory, she should have gradually gained the upper hand in the household; Mrs. C. would then have been reduced to the role of a British sovereign, forced to approve automatically all decisions taken by the government. But Mrs. C. demanded absolute power; she refused to accept reforms. Her reign was not founded on education or a grasp of modern life. Her right to rule was underwritten by a certain style, a certain manner of speaking and dressing (she liked white blouses, washed and pressed by Helena), a certain fussy way of puckering her lips, her four words in French. Knowledge was beside the point. Mrs. C. had no interest in current events. What had to happen had already happened. The notion of following changes in Communist policy and ideology never entered her mind. If someone had told her that there was a real difference between Communism's most brutal year, say, 1952, and the Gomulka period in the sixties, she wouldn't have believed it for a minute. No, she would have refused even to listen.

Helena's rebellions never got off the ground. Mrs. C. didn't suppress them, she simply waited them out. She locked herself up in her little parlor as if it were a fortress, fasted, and patiently waited for the storm to pass. And the storm always did pass. Helena always relented and returned to her endless duties. For a time she would be cross and tight-lipped, but resigned. She would snort angrily and mock everyone who spoke to her, but finally this routine bored even her and, shrugging, she'd regain her usual good nature. Sometimes she took it out on us, the tenants.

She was a magpie, a snoop. I suspected her of regularly rummaging through our things and once left a card that said "Please don't look here" in my desk drawer. Helena took offense and didn't speak to me for several days, and then, when her anger had subsided, she reproached me bitterly: "How could you even think such a thing? So you don't trust me at all."

These two aging women, ugly, taken from a second-rate Dutch painting, hating and tolerating each other by turns, forgiving or forgetting the differences between them, truly existed; brisk, nimble Helena and phlegmatic Mrs. C., pursing her lips. They both went to church on Sunday, but never together. Helena preferred the early mass, while Mrs. C. attended only high mass, carrying a black prayerbook in her right hand and a genuine calfskin handbag in her left.

They lived trapped in a cage, in a second-rate Dutch painting, in a cramped apartment, in spite. I was a student then, attending lectures, everything seemed open, possible. I rushed out of that fourth-floor apartment and instantly forgot the two women's tragedies and hatreds. I paced the path to the neo-Gothic university with rapid steps. I strolled beneath the lush trees of the Planty gardens. At times I pitied the two women, caught once and for all within their little fates. It wasn't fair: infinity was humming right beside them, the stars came out at night. Everything was possible. I heard lectures on Husserl, on Descartes, who'd had his epiphany one night, on Pascal's fire. Some books took flame while others held only straw, clay, feathers. I knew I wouldn't stay long at Mrs. C.'s place, although there were in fact moments when I too took part in the women's dull pain, when their ill humor captured me. These were only moments, though, and I shook them off quickly. But the women were chained to their misery, their inferno; they couldn't break free of it.

Was it naïve to think of them this way? Yes, it was. The jaundiced Mrs. C. couldn't suddenly run from the house and become a young girl yearning for knowledge and revelation. Helena probably couldn't escape the center for rat control.

No, it wasn't naïve. They didn't want a great life. Yes, it was naïve. A great life had been snatched from them forever, for all eternity. Figuring out crossword puzzles—I glimpsed this once completely by chance—was Mrs. C.'s secret. Not a cross, just a crossword. The words marched up and down, but they didn't make sense, they were powerless, crucified. A great nation's capital on a small river. Champagne for children. An African city.

And it had come to this. Mrs. C. had three tenants—two students and a tall old man, already half-dead. Hard of hearing, he listened to the radio for days on end with the volume turned up so high that the walls shook. Of course, he listened only to Radio Free Europe. He moved cautiously, as slowly as possible, shuffling his slippers across the floor. It had come to this: a few pennies in rent, a pension, a cleaning woman's pay.

No, it wasn't naïve, since life is for each of us, for everyone.

I lost two homelands as a child. I lost the city where I was born, the city where countless generations of my family had lived before my birth. But the onset of Soviet-style rule meant I also forfeited my easy, natural access to a general, self-evident truth. It took me many years to return to life's main current, to accept once more the simplest certainties, certainties that only charlatans and madmen call into question.

I came to Krakow to study; it was fall, as it always is when a new school year begins. I came to study, which was praiseworthy and pragmatic, but something else drew me as well. I was propelled

half-consciously by the need to recover my city, the city that had—
and I knew it—been lost forever. But, of course, we always seek
what's gone for good.

I have a photograph of Krakow's city center in front of me; it's an
aerial shot, taken from a plane or helicopter. I found it completely
by accident—the picture was used as the cover of a brochure meant
for foreign tourists. It's graced by stylized letters reading *Cracows
Historic Town Centre* [*sic*]. The English phrase serves a diversionary
function: it distances me from my city, it turns me into a tourist, it
contradicts the obvious fact that I'm looking at something very dear
to me.

The plane, or helicopter, must have been somewhere over
Stradom Street, probably over St. Catherine's Church. I'm not
entirely sure, especially since the stylized English caption obscures
part of the city; it covers the Bernardines' garden and orchard,
reaches the bank of the Vistula, and blocks both the Sports Club
Stadium and the Church on the Rock. The angle of vision coin-
cides almost one hundred percent with a map's distinctive topologi-
cal perspective, that is, with the notion that north is up, west is left,
and east is right. The town center thus resembles a gigantic key-
hole, while the Planty gardens look like the lush green fur collar of
a thriving dentist's wife.

I look at the aerial photograph of Krakow and realize that I'm
the pilot of that plane or helicopter; I'm flying over the city. I'm the
pilot, I'm wearing headphones, and instead of a control panel I've
got an old typewriter, a pen, a pencil, or a slightly outdated computer. I have to wear headphones. The room in which I work, read,
and listen to music—unless I'm in Houston—is located in the belly
of an enormous building. The other occupants generate an ungodly
amount of noise. A housewife paces the kitchen in high-heeled

shoes one floor above me. The kitchen floor is tiled. Every so often one of my countless neighbors renovates his or her apartment, using a drill for this purpose. A drill! The most up-to-date models have the brute force of a tank from the last phase of World War II and are nearly as loud. A drill used even a few floors above me shatters my skull. A drill kills thought and inspiration; it's a bomb exploding inside the building.

Moreover, in front of the building there's a preschool, which an inexhaustible demography restocks every year with a herd of clamorous children, murdering and flirting with one another, imitating their seniors in love and war. One of my neighbors sneezes so loudly that the concrete walls of the building shake. Another has hysterical attacks and screams unceasingly. Each spring the people who live on the other side of the courtyard put a canary out on the balcony, and its soulless, mechanical song is closer to the sound of the drill than to that of the blackbird, the virtuoso among the local wildlife.

I have to wear headphones, and sometimes earplugs underneath the headphones. Only then does my airplane get off the ground. I have to admit it doesn't take off every day. Various obstacles and kinds of interference proliferate; some are external, while others come from within. Sometimes fog on the runway—the runway being my pine desk, purchased years ago for 400 francs in Levallois-Perret—causes flights to be delayed. Other times my plane bumps its nose against the wall right after takeoff, and I miraculously escape with my life, but my ribs and the fingers on my right hand are broken and the nurse smiles sorrowfully. On other occasions snowstorms rage above a different airport, my destination. The radio is also down, my headphones are dead, the transmitter poles have been toppled by the wind, the wires are tangled. What should I do? Jump ship, abandon my post? Read?

I often use the headphones solely as a defense against the trivial, triumphant concert of the commonplace that my colossal apartment house generates. They're a shield, but not quite good enough, they don't get me off the ground, they just protect me from demography and, imperfectly, from the drone of drills. But sometimes it happens that I'm listening to music as my plane circles near the runway, I'm listening to one of Bruckner's symphonies, for example the ninth, whose wild energy could elevate more than one jumbo jet; or Bach, for example his cello suites as played by Janos Starker; or Brubeck, for whom I have a special soft spot since I first listened to him when I was sixteen; or Beethoven, for example the funeral march from the Third Symphony, yes, the one where he erased the dedication to Napoleon so energetically that he wore a hole in the paper; or Mahler's Ninth, with its glorious first movement (*andante comodo*); or Schumann's third piano trio, whose opening movement—*Bewegt, doch nicht zu rasch*—probably doesn't break my heart alone; it promises something it can't deliver, it's as chaotic as desire, as longing, which will never be appeased.

I have headphones over my ears; the typewriter keys, pencil, pen, or computer keyboard are my controls; and the stylized English caption *Cracows Historic Town Centre* sprawls before me, blocking part of the monastic orchard belonging to the Bernardines and encroaching also—I hadn't noticed this before—on the southern fortifications of Wawel Castle. It may not be a plane after all, but a helicopter, since I'm not moving over the city's green Gobelin, I'm hovering in one spot, above the clump of St. Catherine's Church. I don't move over the city, I hover in one spot; the picture must have been taken in midsummer, the town is brown and green, surfeited with light, serene. But no, the tops of some trees are already turning yellow, I see them from above. So perhaps September has already begun, the first week of fall, and only I can see the yellowing treetops, they're still invisible below, for someone looking up it's still midsummer, but for me, far above, the first fine streaks of fall are already visible.

It's late afternoon, nearly evening, the sun slopes westward, the shadows are long and languid, nourished by the sunny day, sated. They've stretched out precisely along the line running east to west, and so run parallel to the churches' elongated bodies, which were, as we know, built upon exactly the same axis, between the sunrise and the sunset, the two most important events of the day.

A bird's-eye view reveals the city's petty secrets, secrets that would be difficult to detect from street level. The view from above resembles a confession, the town admits its venial sins—but not its true, cardinal misdeeds, you have to look for these elsewhere, in memory and forgetting.

I see how many gardens and orchards lie concealed within Krakow's walls. These gardens and orchards are invisible to ordinary mortals, to pedestrians. The high walls shield this priceless green: poplars, ashes, but also apple and pear trees. Some of the gardens cover a fair amount of territory—these are the monastic orchards. A shadow blankets them. The setting sun says goodbye to the town, which has managed to retain its rural nature, but is ashamed of it, and so keeps its green treasures concealed behind the screens of walls and fences. Perhaps it wishes to pass for a modern, cosmopolitan city and doesn't want to acknowledge its idyllically provincial courtyards, the grass that sprouts between the paving stones, the cherry trees blooming blithely in the very heart of the city.

I fly over Krakow lightly, effortlessly, like a spirit. It even seems to me that I feel the warmth of this earth, these rooftops, the lazy warmth of a summer day.

Professor Leszczynski, who had a soft, delicate voice that broke easily, specialized in epistemology. He lectured on Descartes,

Berkeley, Hume, and Kant. He was frail, short, hunched, and meek, with a face so thin that it seemed to be made from plywood, and not from an ordinary, spheroid human body. He was so quiet and mild-mannered he seemed to be living only half a life; he was barely there. He always wore a loden green overcoat, always: in the winter and the summer, for spring and fall, on the street and in the well-heated lecture hall. It didn't matter if a violet-hued Siberian frost had struck, the ruthless frost of Stalin and Beria, or an extravagant, Sicilian heat wave, incapacitating even the greatest athletes—Professor Leszczynski never removed his green overcoat. Students, who see and know everything about their teachers, had an explanation for this phenomenon: Professor Leszczynski had spent some time in Auschwitz and had developed a rare condition there. His inner thermostat had stopped working. Others said no, it hadn't stopped working, it was just that he was always freezing, even in August. But here we bump up against a metaphysical argument: was he freezing, or was he just insensitive to changes in temperature?

But, on the other hand, when I return in my thoughts to Dluga Street now, after so many years, I come to the conclusion that those two ordinary, ugly, aging women, leading the most commonplace, trivial existence, an existence governed by the sluggish rhythm of the seasons, the long, gloomy winter, the frantic spring, the weekly hunt for ham at the butcher's, for carp before the holidays, for stockings in the department store on the Market Square, grudging every penny, hating each other at moments—but never actually going as far as murder!—these two women were more important to the world than I was. They were a better investment for the world, its concern for them bore a higher rate of return than it would ever get from some hotheaded young student. My sudden revelations, my obsession with ancient and modern forms of spirituality were nothing more than a fuse that was already smoldering and might, under the right conditions, set off a bomb! I was potentially one of those fanatics who dream up treacherous utopias, and even if they can't realize them, they're at the very least eager to sign a petition—with both hands!—demanding absolute perfection from the world. And they're convinced that they're right! Those two women, full of anger, weren't looking for radical transformations, and life's unfailing instinct for self-preservation had triumphed in their plain persistence, their tedious battle for survival, the battle to make sure that there was coal in the winter and a poppy-seed cake for Easter. My flights of fancy inevitably contained a touch of scorn for anyone leading a merely normal life: you can scarcely get off the ground without some contempt for ordinary pedestrians! As if a sense of superiority were the essential, high-octane fuel for the imagination's spaceship! I could easily have become the ideal detonator for some demagogue or other. In the gray Poland plundered by the Soviet utopia there was no shortage of cunning petty demons on the party payroll out searching for young souls with ballistic tendencies, souls who dreamed of greatness and despised the trifling daily round of worries and pursuits. Imagination's explosions do ultimately lead to the truth, but its flights come perilously close to the walls of utopia; I've encountered more than one unusually promising young man whose nuptial flight culminated in a grotesque touchdown in the cafeteria of the regional committee of the omnipresent Party.

I lost two homelands, but I sought a third: a space for the imagination, a domain that held room for artistic needs that were still not entirely clear to me. I lost a real city, but I sought a city of the imagination. I picked poetry as my province relatively late, later than many others do.

It might seem as if the inner thermostat of an entire city—Krakow, beautiful, bewitching Krakow!—had stopped working. It cheered the great violinists, David Oistrakh or Yehudi Menuhin, if they happened to visit the local philharmonic, but it was also happy to celebrate someone along the lines of Fidel Castro, who created what was perhaps the most perfect system of police surveillance in human history. Not to mention the petty tributes that the higher functionaries, raised to power by the Party machine, managed to coax now and then from the local population. The city didn't shrink from carefully staged May Day parades, a sneering caricature of spontaneous demonstrations. Nor did it forgo the pseudo-elections in which you tossed into an urn a single card prepared in advance and bearing the names of the lucky candidates: the most primitive robot could have replaced the human hand and brain entirely in performing such a fundamentally mindless function.

The meteorological depressions of Paris have an oceanic feel; the Atlantic dispatches them in the direction of the continent. The wind blows, dark clouds scurry across the city like racecars. The rain falls at a spiteful slant. At times the heavens' face appears, a scrap of blue. And then it's dark again, the Seine becomes a black pavement. The lowlands of Paris seethe with oceanic energy, thunderbolts pop like champagne corks. Whereas a typical Central European depression—centered somewhere above the Carpathians—behaves completely differently: it's subdued and melancholy, one might say philosophical. The clouds barely move. They're shaped differently; they're like an enormous blimp drooping over Krakow's Old Market. The light shifts gradually; the violet glow fades, giving way to yellow spotlights. The sun skulks somewhere behind silken clouds, illuminating the most varied strata of earth and sky. Some of the clouds resemble deep-sea fishes that have ascended to the surface and swim with mouths wide open, as if startled by the taste of air. This kind of weather can last for several days, the meek climate of Central Europe. And if, after lengthy deliberations, a thunderstorm does strike, it behaves as if it were stuttering. Instead of a sharp, decisive shot, it emits a series of drawn-out sounds, *pa pa pa pa*—an echo instead of a blast. Thunder on the installment plan.

Sometimes, as I pass beneath the open windows of a ground-floor apartment, a radio will be playing Elvis Presley or one of his many contemporaries or descendants, hits back in the sixties, but still popular today. And the radio, accidentally overheard, evokes the shrill voice of the electric guitar as I remember it from school dances and student clubs. The shrill, primal sound of the electric guitar, like the voice of a pheasant in the meadow. The electric guitar, morose and sentimental, or at the other extreme, full of sickly vigor, never fails to revive in us that dormant Cartesian question: What is it that keeps body and soul together?

Beautiful, bewitching Krakow. Initiates call it one of our planet's holy places. They say that its castle hill conceals an incalculably precious stone, a rocky talisman possessing magical properties that protect the city from disaster—although reason forces us to confess that it's had its share of disasters. The stone's inner thermostat broke, and it submitted to long years of a gray dictatorship kept in place by bureaucratically gifted Communists.

The birth of a writer: a young man raised in the Catholic faith experiences a dazzling revelation. While praying, he suddenly realizes that he doesn't necessarily have to repeat what's printed in the missal. He can invent his own prayer. He can make up his own words.

I could write a guidebook about this city, this fallen city. Street by street, house by house, church by church. What happened in this building, who was betrayed, and by whom, in this apartment, who waited for whom on this street corner. And why the person never came. I could even play the judge for this occasion and condemn certain acts, censure certain people. I wouldn't lack for material; if need be, I could head for the archives and rummage through dusty files in search of compromising documents. I would be a zealous, incorruptible accuser.

But when I think of years past, when I picture that city, see its inhabitants, the passersby crowding its streets and squares, scurrying or simply strolling, leaping at the last moment onto a moving streetcar or lounging lazily on park benches or in the Planty gardens on a balmy April day, I see myself among them. I was there, too. In the Market Square, on Florianska Street, on Dluga Street; in the old university's lecture halls, in the editorial offices of local journals; I went to theaters, to the movies (most often to the movies, they were exterritorial, Plato's cozy caves and, at the same time, the cheapest travel agencies around, expediting worldwide trips for pocket change), met girls, made a living (just barely). I lived in this city, in Communism, I hopped onto streetcars—as long as they weren't moving too fast. I wrote poems and stories, I started publishing books and anxiously awaited the reviews, I wrote reviews of other people's books. (Young writers behave like public prosecutors hastily appointed by the revolutionary authorities who itch to give respected writers of the older generation the hiding they deserve for their various criminal errors and distortions: all this just in order to survive. It's easier to outlast the trying period of literary youth in a prosecutor's toga than in the defendant's box.)

In the sixties, and later, in the seventies, when I had completed my studies (not without regret), and had to get by somehow, I was fortunate: I wasn't put on trial or thrown into prison, I wasn't harassed by the secret police, and even though I threw myself body and soul into the opposition, I spent only an hour total at the police station. I lived, weeks and months went by, I made various compromises. Now that the era has ended, and those times are over—for good, I hope—suddenly things that seemed completely obvious, though unexpressed, have become difficult to comprehend. What was that lovely city beneath Communism's gray casing? How did it survive? What was transient and what permanent? What still endures and what has gone forever? There are no graveyards for cities, but there is forgetfulness. What was beautiful and what repugnant? Some poems and pictures will live on, but who will revive the moments and hours?

Two wise men once met in a forest clearing. They spoke of the world's poverty, of soulless civilization, of the catastrophic fate that had consumed the inner life, of the downfall of religious feelings. They were in perfect accord: when one spoke, it might just as well have been the other. The silence of the one was the other's silence too. They condemned what needed condemning, and for all the situation's gravity, they secretly rejoiced that neither was alone in this fearful, empty world: the first had the second and the second had the first.

The initial discord arose only that evening, after sunset, as they parted fondly and confided their plans for the next day. I'm going back to the desert, said the first wise man, I'll fast, meditate, spurn the world, and read the classics.

I'll set off for Antioch, the second wise man said, I'll meet people, try to persuade them to my—our—vision, I'll think, write, publish articles and books, and perhaps someone will read them, maybe even be convinced and change his ways. The first wise man looked at him with unconcealed scorn and cold contempt, and vanished into the darkness.

It seems that Professor Leszczynski had never been in Auschwitz, as the students had whispered. But he didn't lack causes for grief; apparently, he'd lost his beloved wife early on. He'd lost his great friend, Stanislaw Ignacy Witkiewicz. He'd lost his fortune, he'd lost an entire world of friendship and thought; he'd found himself after the war in a country as dreary as a barracks. He'd lost his youth.

I can't write Krakow's history, even though its people and ideas, trees and walls, cowardice and courage, freedom and rain all involve me. Ideas as well, since they cling to our skin and change us imperceptibly. The Zeitgeist chisels our thoughts and mocks our dreams. I'm intrigued by all kinds of walls; the space we inhabit isn't neutral, it shapes our existence. Landscapes enter our innermost being, they leave traces not just on our retinas but on the deepest strata of our personalities. Those moments when the sky's blue-gray suddenly stands revealed after a downpour stay with us, as do moments of quiet snowfall. And ideas may even join forces with the snow, through our senses and our body. They cling to the walls of houses. And later the houses and bodies, the senses and ideas all vanish. But I can't write Krakow's history, I can only try to reclaim a few moments, a few places and events; a few people I liked and admired, and a few that I despised.

I'm not a historian, but I'd like literature to assume, consciously and in all seriousness, the function of a historical chronicle. I don't want it to follow the example set by modern historians, cold fish by and large, who spend their lives in vanquished archives and write in an inhuman, ugly, wooden, bureaucratic language from which all poetry's been driven, a language flat as a wood louse and petty as the daily paper. I'd like it to return to earlier examples, maybe even Greek, to the ideal of the historian-poet, a person who either has seen and experienced what he describes for himself, or has drawn upon a living oral tradition, his family's or his tribe's, who doesn't fear engagement and emotion, but who cares nonetheless about his story's truthfulness.

We are in fact witnessing a revival of literature that serves this very purpose, but almost no one's paid attention: writers' journals, memoirs, poets' autobiographies harken back to an archaic literary tradition, the writing of history from the viewpoint of a sovereign individual and not an assistant professor, a slave to modish method-ologies, a state employee who must flatter simultaneously both the powers that be and the reigning Parisian epistemology. Examples? Here's a sampling: the autobiographies of Edwin Muir, Czeslaw

Milosz, Joseph Brodsky, among other poets, the essays of Hubert Butler, Nicola Chiaromonte, the notebooks of Jozef Czapski, Albert Camus . . . The sketches of Zbigniew Herbert, Jerzy Stempowski, of Boleslaw Micinski, ill with tuberculosis. Here are people who refused to cheat, who eagerly sought out the truth and shrank from neither poetry nor terror, the two poles of our globe—since poetry does exist in the world, in certain events, at rare moments. And there's also no shortage of terror.

But that boy who discovered that you can make up your own prayers, you don't always need a prayerbook, would also come to understand with time that a church isn't the only place where you may find divinity.

Witold Gombrowicz's attack on poetry (*Against Poets*) doesn't rank among the harshest accusations leveled against poets in this century. Gombrowicz's essay is more along the lines of a family squabble: the poet-in-prose takes his lyrical brethren to task chiefly for condensing their poems too much, for adding too much sugar to their pastries.

But Gombrowicz's argument deals mainly with poetry's reception, and not with its essence. True, there are periods when poetry seems to offer overly rich fare ("too sweet"). The moments when we're prepared to accept and comprehend poetic intensity come along rarely. But the same is true of painting and music; only film entices us on a daily basis by promising a release from our ordinary indifference.

The English Puritan Stephen Gosson was far more radical, passionate, and primitive in his pamphlet *The Schoole of Abuse*. Gosson argued that poets demoralize the reading public and are in fact no better than rope dancers and wandering actors (and we all know what to expect from them!). Gosson's attack—undertaken in the sixteenth century—would doubtless have been forgotten if it hadn't prompted a far more gifted author to take up the Puritan's charges. This gifted writer was, of course, Sir Philip Sidney, who wrote both verse and prose until his premature death, and who was also one of poetry's greatest champions: his *Defence of Poesie* is a classic of English literature. Sidney defends poetry, inspired poetry—and inspiration is a gift from the gods!—whose finest achievements overshadow those of both philosophy and history. Sidney's treatise, published posthumously in 1595, defends the imagination and insists that it serves good, not evil, ends.

Anyone who's ever been deeply engaged in works of the imagination will know what I have in mind: that moment when, after a long period of immersion, we suddenly bob to the surface and find ourselves stranded in a kind of no-man's-land. The friendly, ardent flames of imagination have abandoned us, but we don't yet stand on the solid ground of everyday common sense. We're suspended for an instant between two spheres that probably converge at some point, but we have no idea where (not in us and not for us). It's a treacherous moment; anyone who starts making lunch or dinner at such a time must take care not to precipitate a fire or even an earthquake.

The most absorbing questions are those we can't answer. Who is man, and by what miracle is he able to transplant his life from one era to the next, from one system to another? And who am I, since I too passed through that sorry era—and I can scarcely claim to have emerged unscathed, calm and pure, internally whole, mature, heroic, uncompromising, uninfected by alien ideas. Now, in hindsight, my defeats and weaknesses defy belief. Could that really have been me? A lecturer at the Institute of Social Sciences, whose goal (the institute's, that is) was unquestionably the ideological bridling of every student to attend the Academy of Mining and Metallurgy. I lectured on the history of philosophy, but my subject was officially called "The Foundations of Marxist Philosophy." My students and I read excerpts from Plato (the defense of Socrates or the allegory of the cave), Descartes' *Meditations*, in which that disembodied philosopher actually describes his fireplace and the room he works in, Kant, Hegel, the existentialists. Sometimes we didn't even make it to Marx, who—in defiance of chronology!—was supposed to crown and conclude the millennial efforts of European philosophy. All the same, I belonged—in name at least—to the army of hirelings sent to subjugate the students' minds.

Once back when I still lived in Gliwice, I dropped in at a bookstore that occasionally stocked books and records from the West. I was about sixteen and devoted to classical music, though I knew next to nothing about it. But I longed to learn more. That day the bookstore happened to have a rarity in stock: Beethoven's complete symphonies under the direction of Herbert von Karajan. They were Deutsche Grammophon recordings with lovely, gleaming covers that featured photographs of von Karajan. The packaging alone was enough to make them art; records produced in Eastern Europe were sold in soiled gray envelopes, and the photos on the covers were bleary and smeared, with misplaced blocks of color.

The salesgirls realized that they'd stumbled onto something exceptional; it even seemed to me that they were smiling with glee, which happened exceedingly rarely. I must have walked in just after this unusual delivery, since all nine symphonies were still awaiting purchasers. I knew they'd be snatched up immediately, all nine symphonies, all nine portraits of von Karajan. It never occurred to me that this was clearly a popular, hence inexpensive, series of recordings. Much later, when I became familiar with the commercial customs of the West, I understood that this handsome conductor's recordings of Beethoven's complete symphonies—or Wagner's overtures—could be picked up in almost any Western European music store.

I also knew that I didn't have much time: other customers would soon appear, some rich lawyer or doctor might take the whole set on the spot. I had to make my choice right then and there, and I had just enough for one record. I couldn't possibly purchase the entire set; that was out of the question, given my modest income.

The Complete Symphonies of Ludwig van Beethoven Under the Direction of Herbert von Karajan must have been relatively inexpensive in the West, but here in the East its price was steep, much higher than that of recordings from Poland, Czechoslovakia, or the Soviet Union, as if crossing the Iron Curtain called for a prohibitive tariff. I could afford only one symphony out of the nine.

To my shame, I knew next to nothing back then about Beethoven's symphonies, only that they ranked among the absolute masterworks of world music. I had nine records in front of me and I had to pick one. I had to take my chances right now, this moment. I suspected that some symphonies might be less wonderful than others, that I might prefer some to others; even genius occasionally nods.

I had only a few minutes. I asked the salesgirl to show me the records. But I couldn't listen to them. I couldn't spend the next eight hours in the bookstore listening to all nine symphonies. It wasn't done. Besides, some rich doctor or lawyer with cultured tastes might suddenly appear, smelling of eau de cologne, and snap up the whole set.

I scrutinized the beautifully packaged records as if I could pierce the music's mystery through layers of cardboard and paper. Looking back, I think the torture I endured then must have been one of

fate's benign amusements; destiny plays tricks on us at times. Perhaps it grows bored during those long interludes when nothing—or
next to nothing—is happening, so it thinks up petty experiments,
little trial runs.

Finally I selected the Seventh Symphony. And within half an
hour I had discovered that Wagner had called it "the apotheosis of
the dance" and that the second movement in particular, the Allegretto, would become one of my favorite pieces of music. Though
years may go by when I don't listen to it (you shouldn't get too
familiar with a piece of music), each time I hear it now I'm as moved
as I was the first time.

I went home, listened to the record, and understood that fortune had smiled on me: I'd picked the right symphony. The seventh. All four movements struck me as beautiful, and not just the
melancholy Allegretto. Those mad dashes that are the Presto and
the Allegro con brio also captivated me. And the first movement,
Poco sostenuto—Vivace, is perhaps the most Beethovenesque of
all, since in it we hear the composer's voice proclaiming the subject
of his epic song, like an ancient poet in his opening canto.

We don't lack for clocks. From my desk I can see at least three
clocks, two electric and one quartz. One is part of my computer and
says it's now 12:29. Another's built into the radio and shows 12:30.
Finally, my wristwatch gives me 12:31. Fortunately, my watch has
traditional hands and doesn't rely upon the ruthless go-betweens of
glowing numerals. We've got a lot of time.

I probably didn't listen to the Seventh Symphony as soon as I got
home. I probably waited a day or two, seized by a superstitious fear

that I'd made the wrong choice. Besides, I must have been over-wrought and needed to wait for the right moment, a moment of calm and concentration.

And at this very moment I'm listening to the Seventh Symphony in Houston, from a recording (Deutsche Grammophon!) entitled *Bernstein: The Final Concert.* Leonard Bernstein, his face marked by illness—the cover bears the conductor's portrait this time too—directs the Boston Symphony for the last time in his life. He wears a white tux. One shot shows him vanishing into the wings. We see him from the rear: a white head set on a short neck, a white tux with black pants. The backstage, a black rectangle, lies before him—the place where the scene ends and the shadows take over.

Mr. Sobertin was friendly with my parents; they may have known each other even before the war. His family was French; before it was Polonized, his last name was probably pronounced with the stress on the final syllable and a nasal "n." He was a tall man, elegantly dressed—you had only to look closely to realize that this was the elegance of another era. I don't remember if he'd had trouble with the police back in the 1950s. But in principle he should have been locked up just for deviating so completely from the model man of the new age. Courteous, beautifully bred, civil to all—how on earth did he survive those times?

He was a bachelor, a gallant gentleman, a troubadour ready to serve any fair lady in the most disinterested and noble fashion. I sensed that he was smitten with my mother, that she was one of his sacred Dulcineas. What struck me most, though, was his manner of taking leave; I made fun of it, after he'd gone, of course. He couldn't allow himself to turn his back on us, so he withdrew with his rear to the door, clicking his heels together repeatedly with an almost military precision. It was irresistibly comic.

Mr. Sobertin should have lived in Provence, not in Communist
Poland. He'd muddled both his epoch and his geography. His forebears had erred by settling in my country.

He was a bachelor in both the new and old senses of the word: a
knight bachelor who'd found neither a wife to settle down with nor
the proper historical moment to inhabit.

His closest friend was the handsome Mr. Cybulski, with his
thick graying mane and bushy brows; he'd lost his wife and child in
the Warsaw Uprising. They often came to see us together, the wid-
ower and the aging bachelor, two mournful men with a melancholy
charm, as if drawn from some old-fashioned deck of cards.

I enjoyed their visits. They didn't stay long, usually just for
afternoon tea and not for supper. Then they'd disappear and return
to the mysterious land inhabited by widowers, old bachelors, cats,
and memories.

A writer who keeps a personal diary uses it to record what he
knows. In his poems or stories he sets down what he doesn't know.

Poets don't particularly fear the onslaughts of Puritan propagandists
or the ferocious attacks that emerge from beneath the pens of their
fiction-writing brethren. The ill will of Jansenists, the wrath of
philosophers who accuse them of following too flighty a muse: neither can do them much harm. The boundless indifference of ardent
TV viewers and fellow passengers on commuter trains is far more
dangerous. It's much worse when no one even bothers to denounce
them.

———

The Alte Pinakothek in Munich holds a portrait of a young
Spaniard by Velázquez; I once spent half an hour in front of that
picture. I felt as though I'd just regained my vision; I could see
again. I suddenly saw a man who lived in the seventeenth century. A
man with a prominent nose (it cast a shadow on his cheek). Enormous eyes. Gloves on both hands, dark garments that bring his face
into relief. His face, deep in thought, is neither ugly nor handsome.
At a certain point I realized that this young nobleman might really
be the devil, hence his exceptional charm (a penitent devil, a devil
seized by fleeting doubts . . .).

One of Rembrandt's earliest self-portraits also hangs there. It's very
small (only 15.5 centimeters by 12.7), and reveals the sensuous face
of a young man who already knows who he is, although he hasn't
yet accepted it (in this he resembles Rimbaud—another brilliant
boy from northern Europe).

Moments of revelation are like boundary stones, separated by several hundred yards of no-man's-land. The poet experiences an
epiphany in setting down the key line of his latest poem. But days,
weeks, even months of shadow stretch between these moments of
majestic clarity. And here the poet plays the historian's role, sharing
not just his ecstatic humanity with his readers but his dull, dreary,
doubting humanity as well.

I'm strolling through Paris. Neither children nor cats pay the
slightest attention to me as I mumble bitterly under my breath.

This is the emigrant's lot. Suddenly I burst out laughing, at myself, at my own exaltation. The children stop short, the cats beat a hasty retreat.

Our spiritual life is shaped by alternating currents of exaltation and demysticization. Since we're now in a period of universal demysticization, we should expect a return to religious dogmatism in the foreseeable future. Which would place me in an awkward situation; I prefer opposing decadence to butting heads with fundamentalists.

". . . You will never love art well, till you love what she mirrors better."—John Ruskin.

This doesn't mean that art, and poetry with it, are simply a mirror held up to reality, as the advocates of realism would have it. No, Ruskin has something else in mind: that art springs from the most profound admiration for the world, both seen and unseen. (And also that it isn't just for aesthetes.)

I like writers and philosophers who know how to rebel against themselves. For example, when someone asked Maurice Barrès near the end of his life what action he was most ashamed of, he said, "That I always voted for my own party." Barrès, an ardent nationalist, nonetheless remarked in *Mes cahiers* that *"nationalisme manque d'infini"*—"nationalism lacks infinity."

Why are detective novels so boring? Because they deal with a single mystery, the simple question of who killed Mr. L. But there's only one real mystery, one real question: What is the world? What is fire? What is air?

French intellectuals love to look down their noses at Americans and their boorishness, their lack of taste. France, which serves the same function in Europe that China does in Asia, frequently fails to understand American enthusiasm. An example: once I was standing before one of the Vermeers in Washington's National Gallery. An American, about forty years old, stood beside me. At one point he turned to me and said (his voice trembled with joy), "I've been looking at reproductions of this painting since I was twenty, and today I'm seeing it with my own eyes for the first time. I'm sorry to bother you, but I had to tell someone."

I can take such lack of culture any day.

Napoleon: *"La force n'est jamais ridicule"* (power is never ridiculous). Napoleon understood this long before Lenin.

Barrès once again: "Cats are like gods—they accept our blandishments, but don't reciprocate."

I had a dream about a writer who was 108 years old. His first great success came at the age of 101. He spoke of it enthusiastically.

Otium as a form of intellectual life undoubtably produced the Buddhists of the late Roman Empire, peaceful souls lost in thought. In his monograph on Saint Augustine, Peter Brown juxtaposes those imperturbable sages to the Christian saint; it's one of his finest observations. Augustine wasn't calm; unlike those scholars who cultivated their stoically unruffled souls while contemplating the letters of Cicero, he was consumed by anxiety and doubts, and by the conquest of those doubts. The path leading to Kierkegaard's anguish lay open.

I realized early on that I'd probably never be a real scholar, an archivist, an academic. I didn't read my way scrupulously through the assigned texts—which weren't just Soviet, hence scarred from birth by the sins of shoddiness, duplicity, and monotony—but also included classics of philosophy. I didn't stroll slowly and sedately through the lanes of printed pages, snaring key quotes with the aid of a pencil before transferring them to a notebook or index cards, the indispensable carapace of the true student. I daydreamed, dropped the book, forgot it, and drifted on to something new, and when I came to, I found myself in another place and time, in Portugal or Chile, on the shores of the Mediterranean, in the Middle Ages or the first decade of the nineteenth century.

And so my assigned reading dragged on at a snail's pace. I never finished anything. I wasn't a good student. Descartes lost patience, Aristotle looked askance. They already knew that this was no young philosopher poring for hours over the pages of their immortal tracts. It was only a poet, a dabbler who couldn't refine a concept or elaborate new nuances in existing categories if his life depended on it. The poet is the philosopher's older brother. Older, but treated for all that with a certain indulgent hauteur; men of learning view him as frivolous, flighty. A person who doesn't spend ten hours a day in stuffy reading rooms can't possibly be taken seriously. A person who makes things up as he goes along. Writes out of thin air instead of cobbling new books from old quotes, footnotes, rereadings of ancient texts. He sits in front of the typewriter with eyes closed, like a clairvoyant. Closer to astrology than to science. He's prone to dubious enthusiasms; at times he sings, laughs, or cries while shut in his own room. True scholars wouldn't do that. Scholars don't close their eyes at their computers. Just the opposite—they prop them open.

This is a beautiful city. It's not a beautiful city. Light as the Renaissance, heavy as lead. It's not an unqualified success; it's not on a par with, say, Tuscany or Lucca (not to mention peerless Florence). Its double nature, ugly and beautiful, heavy and light, befits a land in which architecture generally doesn't work out. Certain individuals may turn out well enough, some sonatas, a few poems. But not buildings, not city planning. Krakow's heaviness often stems from the German influence. In the Middle Ages the German burghers who lived beneath the palace walls of Polish kings and princelings imported the heavy, dark red bricks of the Western Gothic. Later, though, the Polish kings lost their hearts to the Italian Renaissance, with its slim spires, stylish loggias, and vertiginously upright arches. It was as if someone had tied dozens of ether-filled balloons to a massive Gothic trunk and then waited for the stout city, that stony paperweight, to make its way skyward toward the Italian azure. The city never rose, but it changed, grew lighter, double-natured; it sprouted wings.

That's how Krakow seemed to me when I first saw it, in the fall of the year that I left my provincial Gliwice to begin my studies. I

knew it was a beautiful city; everyone in Poland knows that. I
wanted to go to Krakow so I could bask in its authentic antiquity,
experience a place where every generation had left its trace, where
the stones had long kept company with human hands, a place,
moreover, that the last war's bombs had spared. Indeed, Warsaw's
strays had taken shelter here when Warsaw itself ceased to exist,
when the last homes of Warsaw's Old Town had gone up in flames.
What I found in its place was a city fixed in a weary grimace, in the
catatonic stupor of a patient in the psychiatric ward who awaits the
end of the world while clad in his blue-striped pajamas.

The city should have been lovely, but it was disturbingly dark
and dank, full of discordant, dirty spots, and worst of all—this was
fall—it was heaped with little mounds of coal laid by for the winter.
Piles of black and brown coal rose everywhere, like the pyramids of
some pernicious creed that worshipped Darkness. But winter was
on its way and no one could tell what kind of winter it would be. It
might be dreadful: icy, frigid, never-ending. Coal lay on every sidewalk; the rain sifted its black flour and made sure that the dark
water seeped from it in streamlets.

It was a city cluttered with the massive clods of churches and
convents, broad and heavy like aging peasant women gathering
potatoes on a rainy autumn day. The churches had to be heavy,
steadfast anchors, since here Christianity found itself not on a rock
but on boggy, clinging ground. Airy chapels wouldn't do, you had
to build powerfully, to pound your buildings into the damp soil so
that they'd stay put and outlast the winds that gusted from the
world's four corners. The plaster was dark yellow, deep orange,
ocher spattered with gray streaks by the importunate rain. Chestnuts rotted on the pavement, dead leaves towered like Alps on
the Planty gardens' paths. Soot blackened the buildings. Dark,
neglected houses, needing new paint, grew weary of standing on
the same streets. Nothing happened. Whichever street you took,

your downcast eyes saw only the sidewalk's jagged squares, the coal, and grimy puddles. The city's stockings were soiled, its shoes were caked in mud. The smell of autumn leaves, as ambiguous as annihilation, smoke from the occasional bonfire, as someone burned weeds and rubbish: these improved things, made amends, and you forgot the blackened sidewalk for a moment. The smell of the bonfires was intoxicating, narcotic. Summer's memory was burning, leaves and stalks burned, the stalks of those same leaves that we greet with pious awe each April, and then reduce to ashes come September or October. Such prodigality, such potlatch, such hallucinosis lurked in that low-lying smoke, hanging motionless just over the city like telephone wires. The squat apartment houses, run-down taverns, tradesmen's dwellings, even the occasional palace—all had a vaguely Hungarian air, as if the German and Italian influences had given birth to a provincial, Magyar Baroque.

Fall was cold that year, evenings came on early, dusk fell, the poplars' dry leaves quivered, dreading November and the first frosts. So much grayness and dirt; night reluctantly made way for drowsy, dreary days that scarcely deserved their places on the calendar. Those who were alive just went on living. Those who weren't stayed strictly out of sight. But even the living were eager to keep a low profile. If you had an apartment, you stayed home, avoided going out, as if this were some northern settlement perched just beyond the Arctic Circle. For all that, though, everyone knew that you had to endure, keep living at any cost. Everything was geared toward survival, vegetation. That's how it was, that's how things were done. Some very old women, two hundred years old at least, spent their days out of doors, wrapped in ancient wool rags and newspapers as they sold onions and cabbages shriveled with cold, or simply begged. Everyone else took shelter in their apartments, beneath the orange lampshades of warm lights, huddled by tiled stoves glimmering with every color of the rainbow. It might have been the nineteenth century, so little had changed. It was cold. The goal was not to go out at all, not to leave the apartment. Outside there was Communism and frost, or if not frost, then a ceaseless, teasing drizzle that further dirtied the walls. Nowa Huta and Skawina kept emitting their poisonous fumes; you were better off just staying home.

The town was lovely just the same. Its Renaissance lightness lifted it above the autumn's sordid mud, above the rain's never-ending *sfumato*. A few drops of Renaissance sufficed to lift the city, to subdue the murderous inertia of its bulky buildings. Heavy as lead, light as the Renaissance. It was always besieged by its bulk, like an elderly lady waging a desperate battle with her weight. It was besieged by autumn and filth and gray streaks on the walls, and by its outsized share of alcoholics. In dark moments, it seemed as if Krakow were populated exclusively by drunks, prowling the streets with their eternal, unchivalrous cry: Son of a bitch, son of a bitch. If not for those drops of Renaissance, Krakow would have perished in the swamp, sunk to the bottom like so many other dreary cities muttering in an idiot's guttural voice: Fucking son of a bitch . . .

But here in Krakow squares blossomed, the Old Market opened its expanse, you could escape the tangle of alleys, arches, balconies, and courtyards and make your way into Renaissance daylight, drink your fill of fresh air that sometimes held a presentiment of spring.

That was my first autumn in this city, a cold and rainy autumn. It seems to me that I remember every single day. I recall the acrid smell of moldering leaves, the bonfires' sweet scent, the dirt and drowsiness of certain streets. But the city astonished me, I was enthralled, since I discovered here a continuity of life unbroken by the war. It was 1963, I was eighteen years old. My first lodgings in Krakow were on Dluga Street.

———

Last night we heard again, for the second time, a wonderful, very young Hungarian violinist who played in a style that fused traditional Gypsy songs (although he's thin and fair) with classical music and jazz. This violinist—his name is Lajko Felix—has an extraordinary command of his instrument. He improvises effortlessly, with a rhythm and speed that take your breath away. But this is no virtuoso, whose flawless technique serves only to stun stern critics into silence. He performs not in sterile, silent concert halls but in cafés filled with the clatter of cups and glasses and catering to an incorrigible clientele completely unversed in music, patrons whose chief passion is foolish banter. He wouldn't think twice about playing in railway stations and crowded restaurants, even football stadiums. This choice is significant; it bears witness to the academic and commercial character of the music industry in our times. The freshness of performing—and listening—is lost in the rustling of banknotes and carefully drawn-up, easily broken, contracts. Often young musicians—I'm also thinking now of an informal concert staged by young students at Krakow's Mozart Academy in 1994—play with far greater passion than older, wealthier artists. Unfortunately, young musicians invariably become old ones over time.

The young violinist's artistry even makes me laugh at times; it reminds me yet again that laughter is sometimes the best answer to art's perfection.

Bread, house, salt, God—the family of simple, monosyllabic words.

A few years ago a huge German-Polish conference was held in Cologne, attended chiefly by businessmen and politicians. But they also invited a small group of Polish writers in order to add a splash of color to the gray suit of legitimate economic discussion. I didn't quite know what I was supposed to discuss with this crowd. So I talked about—what else—Polish poetry. It still holds a spark of an ancient, magical vision of the world, which must also be the vision of the future, that is, if we want the world not simply to survive but to retain some semblance of spiritual health. The Polish ambassador to Bonn, a charming man, took the floor just after me. He extolled a modern Poland, an up-to-date, rational country emphatically open to every kind of economic reform the West could offer. I realized that I'd committed a faux pas; I'd been acting like a shaman, a reactionary. I'd been glorifying magic.

Try to imagine a time when the *Divine Comedy* had not yet become an awe-inspiring monument of world culture but existed only as a work in progress. Dante's busy writing, say, the Fourth Canto and anything could happen; he could catch pneumonia and die before the end of the *Inferno*. He's already got a vision of the whole in his head, but there's still a long and treacherous road to tread before it's all safely down on paper. Bacteria and viruses don't sleep—to say nothing of political opponents.

I like to think of that moment, and not just for philological reasons. In some sense the world is always in the position of this unfinished manuscript, even if we don't see any masterpiece in progress at the moment.

When asked if European music has a core, that is, if one work or another might be called its heart, B. answered, "Yes, of course, the aria 'Erbarme Dich' from Bach's *Passion According to Saint Matthew*."

At first I majored in psychology, but I soon grew disillusioned—it dealt only with the "how," and not with the "what." So I switched to philosophy, where I hoped to find meatier fare.

In childhood, some trees murmured even on windless days.

Opinions, notions, concepts: they're not enough, even when we embrace them with all the force of an intellectual passion. They always stand in need of correction (we ourselves will begin to eye them suspiciously within a few years), someone always appears who isn't swayed by our seemingly flawless arguments, who starts picking holes in them, who counters them (horror of horrors) with his own notions and opinions. This is why an essay shouldn't be smooth, like the face of a newly polished mirror; it should bristle with thorny metaphors, with the weeds of epic arrogance and imagination, which want the world more than the truth (though I believe in truth!).

He asked: You haven't gone back to Y.'s book for a couple of years, why not, it's a wonderful book, we could all learn something from it.

Of course, it's true, I've been thinking about that too. Here's
what happened. I put a Latin dictionary I hardly ever use on the
same shelf, and it covered Y.'s book up. And that's the only reason it
slipped my mind.

In search of two lost homelands—one a city, the other free access to
the truth—I stumbled upon a third, without even knowing that I'd
ever lived there. It doesn't command much territory and has no
army; it holds only a small spring that reflects the blue sky and a few
frayed white clouds.

But this third country possesses one peculiar trait: every now
and then it vanishes from the face of the earth. For long stretches at
a time. It disappears like swallows flying south, who leave behind
only archaic nests beneath the eaves, the roofs' little chins.

Johann Sebastian Bach had, if memory serves, twenty children from
two different marriages (not all survived to adulthood, as was often
the case before our hygienic age). Our contemporary Glenn Gould,
who wanted to do Bach justice, sentenced himself to total isolation.

Professor Leszczynski belonged to a family that officially didn't
exist. The omniscient regime just barely tolerated them. It kept a
close eye on them, watching even their fingers and lips. A person
like Leszczynski recalled a chess piece kept in permanent check. He
could give his seminars and lectures, but pains were taken to make
his topics as abstract and uninviting as possible.

Perhaps Professor Leszczynski's perennial loden coat was meant to protect him from this permanent check. Something like the magic invisible cap in fairy tales.

Someone who defends poetry and magic can't afford to scorn reason or even common sense. In our world, the world of computers and the free market, reason and common sense occupy a privileged place. But a person defending poetry begins from a weaker base and can't—shouldn't—take leave of his senses so completely as to advocate the abolition of reason. He hopes at best to negotiate a modified status quo: more room for imagination, more tolerance for dreams and magic.

But it's not just a question of respecting reason for its superior strength; reason orders our collective existence, protects it from folly.

The Institute of Philosophy was housed in a building on what was then called the Street of the July Manifesto (Pilsudski has reoccupied it since): Number 13, First Floor. The Institute of Psychology was on the second floor, Teachers' Training occupied the third, and the pedagogues and psychologists divvied up the fourth floor's lecture halls between them. Professor Emeritus Stefan Szuman, the glory of prewar psychology, a humanist and connoisseur of painting and music, also lived on the top floor. Before the advent of the new system, he'd headed the psychology department. Now he was merely—could only be!—a living reproach to the current potentates, those professors who meekly curried favor with the state. Szuman wasn't a Marxist, so the system had no use for him; he was transferred to the attic and relieved of his academic duties. And they'd found a convenient pretext: he'd reached retirement age.

A short, stout, balding man, Szuman had befriended Witkacy before the war, and he'd also known Bruno Schulz. Schulz wrote a series of rather unctuous letters to Szuman, who was already a well-known intellectual when Schulz began the correspondence. Schulz himself was still unknown. A provincial artist and writer teaching crafts at the Drohobycz Academy, he sought the support of someone who'd already made a name for himself. But all we saw was a plump, poorly dressed old man struggling to get his groceries up the stairs; now and then we'd catch sight of the shoots of an onion or the stiff stem of a leek poking from his shopping bag. Sometimes his wife, also elderly, was with him. The pair would mount the stairs slowly, with long pauses on every landing. They didn't look at us. They didn't look at anything. They held sorrow, poverty, age. Their violated intimacy, mundane purchases, and shabby clothes had ceased to shame them. We—I mean "we students," since individuality grew faint, faded away there on the collective-minded stairs of Philosophy and Psychology—didn't pay much attention to them either, a fat old man and a skinny old lady with thin gray hair. They were too distant from us, too different, too old.

To them, on the other hand, to Szuman and his wife, we must have seemed like barbarians, shaped by a postwar education, by new schools, new papers, new radio, TV. We must have looked like fools, savages, products of the new system who knew only Lenin, who had never read Slowacki or Dante, had never heard of Sophocles and Leonardo da Vinci. And if we had, it could only have been secondhand, by way of the new textbooks in which the forces and conditions of production gave birth to artists and artworks in a dry, mechanical, clockwork fashion entirely lacking in eros and passion. The progeny of such parents could only be stillborn: still lifes, dead symphonies and epics, mercenary soldiers, and venal geniuses.

We may have frightened them, who knows? That herd of twenty-year-old intellectuals must have looked like athletes, discus throwers, sprinters to an old couple worn from wandering. Every careless gesture must have threatened their fragile equilibrium. We were so distant! The two generations severed by time might have passed for citizens of different countries. We shared no common territory, had no ground for dialogue, discussion, understanding. The Szumans had witnessed and taken part in the complex culture of interwar Poland, a culture obsessed (and rightly) with the prospect of calamity, annihilation. We students, on the other hand, were absorbed in our own youth (though our author wasn't Lenin but Kafka, who also dealt chiefly with catastrophe). Two worlds, two planets, so it seemed, two continents that would never meet. It looked as if the system had won. It had segregated youth from age in a typically perverted way. It quarantined us from the finest members of the interwar intelligentsia by allowing frequent contact there on the stairs, a purely physical contact that not only didn't prompt dialogue but actually made it impossible.

But the generations made contact just the same; they kept in touch, passed messages, established an exchange. It wasn't exactly a dialogue—twenty-year-olds don't usually have much to say, at most a few biting comments on the best-known figures of the day. There was genuine contact, though, not so much on that staircase, on those stairs where no one lived and everything smelled of oil paint and floor wax massaged into the parquet by an army of cleaning ladies. The real contact took place in the libraries.

I didn't pay much attention to the Szuman I physically encountered on the staircase; my interest proceeded more obliquely. It's hard to speak of love or even sympathy; I didn't feel any affection for Stefan Szuman personally. It was enough for me that he'd known Witkacy and Schulz and probably Irzykowski and other people who'd been personally acquainted earlier on with Stanislaw

Brzozowski—and they were my heroes, the authors of my favorite
books, the secret companions of those afternoons in the library when
I shoved my boring psychology texts aside and lost myself in poems,
essays, novels. Old Szuman's stock would suddenly shoot skyward in
my eyes the minute that I recalled his friendship with these writers.

I'd try to imagine his meetings with those geniuses, his talks
with Witkacy, his first contact with Schulz. I'd try to summon up
that whole vanished culture, killed off by the Germans and Russians, the large apartments with paintings on their walls, the vast
bookcases, and most of all the clear sight and free souls of people
who had chosen their own convictions, who had handpicked their
pessimism, people who didn't yet live in the shadow of that moloch,
the one and only all-consuming Party. They still had a choice. Few
of them embraced Hitler's or Stalin's violent, hysterical solutions as
had so many of their contemporaries elsewhere in Europe. Poland's
grim atmosphere in the thirties didn't lead them to become apolo-
gists for the status quo, persuaded that the prevailing reality is
rational by definition.

I imagined their debates, their arguments, even their dreams, in
which the coming catastrophe, the future horror of war, camps,
humiliation, hunger, must have spoken to them in the enigmatic
tongue of signs and parables. (Their dreams were probably quite
different; there's freedom even in the land of dreams.)

Now, of course, I know that I should have gone up to him,
crossed the border that had been artificially drawn between generations, I should have asked him for a chat, since that might have
encouraged him, given him some hope that the oblivious students
racing up and down the stairs actually did know something about
him and his friends. They knew of Witkacy's despair and his suicide; they knew he'd died not because he feared for himself but
because he knew that civilization was doomed, he saw the coming
finis mundi; they knew that on his deathbed he'd dragged every-

thing he'd ever known or read into oblivion, he died with Sophocles and Calderón, Petrarch and Kochanowski, he took with him
the entire memory of enlightened humanity. And they knew that
Szuman, his friend, had survived the world's end and had come
to know a bitterness perhaps even greater than the sorrow of Witkacy's final days, greater than the *finis mundi*, the bitterness that
tainted the days, weeks, and months of his old age.

He climbed the steep stairs every day clutching his heavy sacks
of potatoes and cabbages, and he had to make peace with the fact
that they'd turned him into a freak show, the man-monkey, the
bearded lady, someone subjected against his will to the hostile or
mocking gaze of a younger generation, someone forced to display
himself in all his helplessness, to show his well-worn coat, his aging,
shapeless body to an amused or apathetic public. I should have gone
up to him, he might have been less frightened, his loneliness might
have lightened, if he'd been able, if only for a moment, to make
contact with someone so much younger than himself. He would
once again have become a creature with a mind and soul, not some
deeply flawed physical specimen.

But I never did approach the old professor, I never started up a
conversation—at least until now, long since, when I'm no longer
young myself, and it's too late.

In one of Paris's cafés they've hung a sequence of photos showing
the Eiffel Tower at different stages of construction: at first you see
only four enormous paws sprouting from the earth, then an awkward torso thoughtlessly lopped off at the waist. And finally, in the
very end, the giant mantis rears its tiny head.

———

Treasures: he asked them over. I'd like to show you my treasures, he said. I have vast treasures at my house.

They drove along a river gleaming in the sun. They didn't speak: he was silent from suppressed joy, awaiting the moment when he would reveal his treasures, while they were puzzled or perhaps merely worn out from the trip.

When they got out of the car, he went ahead, gesturing.

But the house was empty. No treasures in sight. An ordinary house. The refrigerator murmured in the kitchen, while in the dining room the TV dozed with the pale face of a sickly child. The books stood unmoving on shelves, as if glued to the walls.

The guests were tactful and avoided painful questions. But it was clear that they were disappointed. They left unhurriedly, praising the silence that filled the house.

That at least, at least that much.

He said good night and clumsily made his excuses, apologizing for the confusion.

Then he sat on the floor for a long time, staring out the window. Poplar branches shifted slowly; perhaps the wind was blowing, or maybe it was just birds playing in the leaves.

After a little while he almost forgot what had happened. And the treasures came back. The house was full of treasures once again.

The nineteenth-century playwright Friedrich Hebbel is still performed, though rarely, in the German theater. His intellectual diaries have ensured his immortality. The critic and novelist Karol Irzykowski, whose work I studied so devoutly as a young man, was a scrupulous reader and translator of Hebbel's diaries. One of Hebbel's greatest aphorisms is also the epitaph on his tomb: "If a tree wilts, if only at the crown, it's just because the roots aren't deep enough. The whole world is its possession." This last sentence is astounding. The whole world is its possession. And yours. And mine.

While Hölderlin says: *Aber der Baum und das Kind suchet, was über ihm ist.* But the tree and the child seek what is above them.

Before I started studying philosophy, though, or rather, before I started to pretend that I was studying philosophy, I'd done psychology. That was my first choice, linked more to the city that housed the university, to Krakow, than to the course of studies. I didn't care what I majored in, as long as it was the humanities. I wanted to be a writer in any case (even though I hadn't written anything yet, I was still "getting ready to write"), but you couldn't major in creative writing, as in the United States, so what else was there? Polish literature? I was afraid that the academic scholarship, with its pedantry, would kill my love of reading, the dilettantish fervor, the amateur's unprofessional enthusiasm that I hoped to retain for a lifetime. My main goal was to leave provincial Gliwice and end up in Krakow. To live in a genuine city at any cost. I told myself that psychology couldn't do any harm, I wanted to be a writer, some knowledge of psychology might come in handy. I'd conceal my real calling, I told myself, my dreams of writing, I wouldn't let on, wouldn't show that my heart lay elsewhere, that my attitude toward psychology was a little cynical. I could probably use it for something. I'd soon think differently; but I didn't know that yet.

I began by attending the opening-day ceremonies on October first, which were held, as always, in the assembly hall of the

Collegium Novum, a neo-Gothic edifice trying to pass for the real thing. I arrived late, the little hall must already have been overflowing, the crowds oozed onto the small square out in front. So I stood beneath the bare sky, like one of the peasants outside a church, the peasants who don't exactly believe but still feel compelled to visit the local shrine come Sunday. But they also need to show that they've kept their manly strength and independence, not like their wives, who press against the altar. In my case, though, it was just garden-variety lateness; I wouldn't have minded squeezing into the hall to see the venerable academic senate decked out in its ermine and togas.

I bumped into two students whom I recognized from the entrance exams in early July, before vacation. So we stood together, another student and a beautiful girl whom I remembered very well from the exams. We stood together, bound by a shared future; we knew we'd see each other often in the coming years. Our names began with "W" and "Z," we were the alphabetical rear guard, and that drew us together. Thus far we knew each other only from that stuffy little hall where we'd spent three or four hours last July scribbling endless essays on Polish literature: this had been our ponderous introduction to the intricate ritual of entrance exams. We spent most of our time then staring at the sheets of paper that were meant to contain our essays, but we glanced up curiously at one another too. We'd come to know each other much better during our studies, and much, much later that girl would become my wife.

On February 15, 1853, a failed attempt was made on the life of the Austrian Emperor; this was the long-lived Franz Josef I, whose likeness adorns my favorite paperweight, which belonged once to Aunt

Lusia, my grandfather's half-Germanized sister. Shortly afterward, the poets of Austria were ordered to write verses commemorating the Emperor's miraculous escape.

There are two attitudes that you can take to the world. You can side with the tight-lipped skeptics and cynics who gleefully belittle life's phenomena, reducing them to a series of minute, self-evident, even commonplace components. Or, option two, you can accept the possibility that great, unseen things do exist and, without resorting to lofty rhetoric or the intolerable bombast of itinerant Bible-thumpers, you can try to express them, or at least pay them tribute. This doesn't mean shutting your eyes entirely to everything little and low.

One of my uncles—I had no lack of uncles and aunts in Krakow!— was a retired veterinarian. He lived in a lovely spot, right by the Stary Theater, in a well-maintained, traditional apartment (one of those "old Krakow apartments" that the less fortunate Poles living in cities destroyed by the war always spoke of with longing and envy). The only catch was the elevator, which had been out of order for years, and my aunt and uncle—just like Professor Szuman, whom they'd certainly never met—lived on the highest floor. Elevators could not be fixed: a fatal flaw of the new regime. Once something broke, it stayed broke.

My aunt and uncle expended a great deal of time and energy just trying to reach their floor. They were consoled only by the rather elegant benches that stood at every turning of the staircase, like tents on Himalayan slopes. You could catch your breath there. It was a long journey.

Later, as they grew older, they were completely cut off from the world. Only the services of the young student they'd hired saved them. She brought them their groceries, their papers, and gusts of a younger, fresher life. It hadn't yet come to that, though, when I used to visit them in Krakow. Their apartment became a hermitage only gradually; my uncle's problems with his legs came on over time.

He liked to show me photos of the famous people whose pets he'd tended. A picture of a lovely, laughing Basia Kwiatkowska hung on one wall. He was a veterinarian who genuinely liked animals, even pigeons. The plague of cities even then, pigeons found favor in his eyes, the eyes of a gifted veterinarian. My aunt once told me that while he could still walk, he'd feed the pigeons with a mixture of grain that he'd sprinkled with antibiotics. Pigeons get so sick sometimes . . .

He was in the habit of adding the phrase "Wouldn't you know it" to every sentence. "Wouldn't you know it, she died in October." "And then I, wouldn't you know it, caught a cold."

And wouldn't you know it, he died too.

Inscription on a gravestone found in North Africa: "I, a captain in the Roman legions, have thoroughly considered the following truth. There are only two things in life, love and power, and no one can have them both at once."

Good writers package the unknown in the known. Bad writers put the unknown up on top.

———

Wiktor Woroszylski died in Warsaw a few weeks ago. An honorable man, and a good, courageous poet. He was one of the totalitarian regime's most stalwart opponents in the seventies. He founded and edited the first major underground journal (*Zapis, The Record*), and he encouraged those who were younger and less experienced than himself. I mention the seventies, since that was when I met him and encountered his work in the opposition firsthand. But it had begun much earlier, in the mid-fifties. His critiques were brilliant and sometimes scathing. His views on the system and its slaves carried great weight; they devastated their targets, crushed them. His personal experience of Russia—he'd witnessed both the splendors and the shame of its intellectuals and writers—enriched his vision. He was a champion of freedom, and the scorn that colored his judgment at times was just the flip side of his love for liberty, a passion that's difficult to put into positive terms. Since what can you say: I love liberty? I'd do anything for freedom? Tact didn't permit him to indulge in such truisms, and these sentiments took the shape, instead, of censure, even mockery. They also informed his own actions, needless to say.

Yet this extraordinary man had early on ranked among the most ardent adherents of a system he later came to loathe. He was one of those rabid young poets whom the party used like a pack of hounds to track down older writers suffering from reactionary lack of faith in the one true cause. They didn't pursue only writers who said nothing, who stood on the sidelines. They also attacked writers who supported the cause, but halfheartedly, who didn't take Mayakovsky as their model. (Woroszylski wrote a wonderful book on Mayakovsky much later.) Wiktor belonged to this group of young zealots, the bane of so many older writers. And the bane of every decent, thoughtful person. And a plague to the muses too, who were baffled by such fanatics and had no idea what to do with them.

And this was the same person I came to know years later, one of the noblest men I've ever met. He wasn't a heel, a hustler looking to line his own pockets. And he wasn't a graphomaniac, just a talented poet, one of fortune's young favorites, born to speak out. And this high-minded, decent man was able, however briefly, to turn on literature itself, to become an anti-literary terrorist! It's unnerving— we're so weak, so prone to give the era what it wants to hear, to follow its promptings, to heed the dictates of the Zeitgeist. When we're young, we're as delicate as hemophiliacs; even the slightest injury may prove fatal.

In certain poems we feel as though we've gotten lost, gone astray. But we're not afraid, not even in the way that certain dreams may frighten us. I'll copy out the first stanza of an early lyric by Quasimodo (only his early poems have this quality). The poem is called "Gentle Hills":

> Distant birds open to the evening
> tremble over the river. The growing rain
> throws light on poplars groaning
> in the wind. All forgotten things
> return. The soft green
> of your gown mingles with the green
> plants born of thunder. The gentle hill
> of Arden Forest rises and we hear
> kites cry above the buckwheat's fan.

Quasimodo later became a "socially engaged" poet and his verses lost their almost spectral lightness; they lost the quality that quietly lures us into the wilderness, that sets us adrift amid the poem's pastel plants and crying birds.

The young Hofmannsthal tempts us even more exquisitely, especially in his prose. In the *Cavalry Tales*, for example, he unveils the world's chaos for a moment, reveals a spot where the world ruptures, where there is no solid land, no sand, no water, only fissures. He does this so skillfully, though, that we don't have time to ask why or how, and the brutal, much abused word "absurd" never even comes to mind. More than this: we're entranced by his anarchy (momentarily, at any rate; we wouldn't want to spend our lives there).

The stone, the magical stone that's supposedly concealed within the Wawel Castle hill, draws sightseers. You always see a few people standing outside the palace, in the castle's courtyard, with their palms pressed against the wall, waiting for the moment when their skin will absorb the stone's hidden energies.

I visited Krakow's libraries. Early on, I made do with modest, minor collections: the great Jagiellonian Library unnerved me at first. Constructed in a modern, functional style during the thirties, it was part of the architectural legacy bequeathed to Krakow by the Second Republic. Its vast main reading room, with its endless tables and lamps, would become my sanctuary later on. I came here to escape my cozy little room at Mrs. C.'s, and the roommate who shared it with me. The library's expansive anonymity preserved me from unwelcome intrusions. I almost always ordered two different kinds of books; some were meant to please my professors, the philosophers and psychologists, while others were just for me. The first type were textbooks, the second type held poems, stories, essays. These books were what I took up first, they swallowed me. The textbooks oozed boredom, I read them because I had to. (You should keep in mind that back then a psychology student was forced to plod through Soviet texts, translated from the Russian: for example, the infamous tome of one Rubenstein, a specialist in mechanical dialectics, master of the miniaturized Hegelian triad, and tawdry peddler of analysis and synthesis.) These two categories belonged to entirely separate cultures. I had to check my watch in order to tear myself away from the books I loved and scrounge a few minutes to scribble notes on the boring books for whatever course or seminar I had next. Heaven and earth, these two sets of books. The bad ones were written in a completely different language: flat, wooden, expository, and frequently false. The others, though, were ardent, infused with inspiration. It wasn't just a question of prose versus poetry, mind over metaphors. The good books didn't lack for thoughts, but the ideas sprouted with the imagery. The language wasn't the dull, indifferent speech of a court reporter: it warmed and grew just as the book did. The language in them was a living entity; it made my heart beat more powerfully. These books spoke to me. They said that I too might follow the same routes one day, that I too might pilot such aircraft. But I also knew it wouldn't be any time soon, that the most I could hope for was grotesque hops and starts like those that met the Wright Brothers' first efforts.

The limits of the spirit: a comic episode that André Gide describes in great detail in his diaries of 1942–43. The venerable writer, the toast of European literature, arrives in Tunis. He's staying at the place of some friends, but the friends are out of town, and only their son and his grandmother (whom Gide calls Chacha in the diaries) remain at home. Victor is fifteen, Gide is seventy-three. Victor is a teenager, Gide is a colossus of modern French prose. Tunis, which had for many years been spared by war, suddenly becomes the locus of military actions; German and Italian divisions occupy the city, while the surrounding American forces bombard it. At the same time, of course, a ferocious war drags on in Russia, on the Eastern Front. But Gide is temporarily beset by other troubles. The fifteen-year-old Victor turns out to be a more powerful personality than the aging writer. Ruthless, egotistical, miserly, and idle, he terrorizes his grandmother and declares all-out war on the author of *Lafcadio's Adventures*.

Lafcadio existed only on paper and had to take orders from his maker. But the fifteen-year-old Lafcadio from Tunis stops at nothing. He's a model egotist. He gobbles up the finest morsels—and this with besieged Tunis facing famine! He demands payment for the smallest service. And he openly despises the elderly writer. He's no fool, he's read Rousseau and Diderot, but he doesn't betray the slightest trace of admiration for the famous author who shares his roof.

The war with Victor apparently absorbs Gide more than the real war being fought outside his door. The Allied forces slowly gain the upper hand over the Axis, but Victor emerges triumphant from the scuffle with Gide. He's self-assured, he is seemingly immune to human feelings, and he feels no scruples about his triumphant skirmishes with Gide. Who just keeps on writing it all down.

It sometimes bothers me that I made my debut as an angry young man, a political poet dead set against the system. Such poetry ceased to interest me long ago. I understood that true poetry lay elsewhere, outside the improvised battle plans of political parties, beyond the reach of even the most righteous revolt against tyranny. But back then, in the late sixties and early seventies, I probably couldn't have done otherwise. We—I have in mind the young poets who emerged at that time—had ourselves been infected with the system's poisons. In glancing through my notebooks from the seventies, I catch traces of my ostentatious enthusiasm for various leftist readings and clichés—I studied writers like Gramsci, for example, the so-called enlightened Communists. I managed to free myself from them at moments, but by and large I seem to have been completely under their sway. All writers should be obliged to scrutinize the idiots of both persuasions, left and right. The poet is a born centrist; his parliament is elsewhere, and houses both the living and the dead. This is why poets should always endorse a parliamentary system with an expanded unicameral legislature.

In opposing the system, our poetry helped to free us from reflex leftism, from pervasive falseness; it was autotherapy. We obeyed the dictum: *Medice, cura te ipsum.* Perhaps we performed the same function for some of our readers at times. And our concern for the concrete particulars of everyday life was bracing; we broke with a tradition of modernist hermeticism that didn't permit much by way of active engagement with history.

Shelley also took the poet's part in his famous *Defence of Poetry,* in which he refers to Sidney. His definition of poets as the unacknowledged legislators of the world is still in common currency today, although it's ordinarily quoted with a slightly embarrassed smile.

We talked about growing older at a friend's house yesterday. One friend will soon be turning sixty, which depresses him. We talked about youth and the way that commercial art, film for example, holds no room for age. Someone had written a screenplay in which a thirty-seven-year-old woman has a passionate love affair. The producer said, "She's too old. Thirty-two tops."

But growing old isn't a tragedy as long as your mind stays supple, the world's spectacle still engages you, your curiosity doesn't flag. No abyss divides youth from age. The real abyss lies between the living and the dead. And the greatest barrier of all separates those who've never been born from those of us who've had a taste of existence.

When they announced the prophet contest, I applied, convinced that I belonged to the dwindling tribe of truly spiritual souls, and shouldn't shrink from my preordained mission. I got through my exams pretty well, I thought, and three days later, I had an interview with the chair of the selection committee, a small man with an enormous head.

Good intentions aren't enough, he said. Your theoretical exams weren't bad, although you still need some work on the New Testament. But your taste for halftones, your muted voice, your smiles and asides—they put you completely out of the running. You lack wrath!

Downcast, I left the dilapidated building and ran into a janitor. He took me aside and whispered conspiratorily: They're holding a prophet contest, but they don't have a clue about what a prophet's really supposed to do. They wanted to find out from the applicants, from you! From schoolboys! They haven't got a clue.

A blunt, straightforward style too often leads to a deceptive triviality; Marek Hlasko is one such instance. A high style, on the other

hand—Ernst Jünger would be an example—takes us in the opposite
direction, toward an equally false ostentation. Writers who employ
such languages have to recognize that sooner or later they'll end up
in a trap that's set for them by their very style.

The literature of the last two hundred years—or even longer!—
abounds in abusive portraits of the middle class, the bourgeoisie.
Is there anything they haven't done? Your average bourgeois
is miserly, mean-spirited, egotistical, small-minded, incapable of
self-sacrifice, heroics, devotion. Writers have found their ideal
scapegoat in this philistine. What's more, these spiteful attacks
strike home; as often as not they're right. With one small quali-
fication—they describe not the bourgeoisie so much as humanity generally, *Homo sapiens* in his only authentic incarnation.
"Bourgeois" is a marvelous pseudonym for the human race as
such. Both writers and readers are happy: neither sees himself in
that ghastly monster who takes off his glasses, sets down his
book, and steps out for a brisk constitutional in the best of
humors.

Passersby always stop to see a puppy who's gleefully discovering the
world. A young dog who'll jump on anyone, lick any palm, who
hasn't quite mastered his legs yet—he moves us through his very
awkwardness, which stems from an overabundance of energy
and not decrepitude. It's tonic. No one goes up to old dogs, though.
Old dogs have a hard time moving at all. Old dogs stricken with
rheumatism sometimes move sideways, like crabs. Old dogs with
ailing backs are kept up, even carried, by their leashes (the same

leashes that were used to rein in restless puppies not so long ago have turned into life preservers). Old dogs move slowly. Not only do they lack the strength for walks; they clearly don't even like them. It's just the doctor's orders that condemns them to this torture. Old dogs pay no attention to puppies. And nobody looks twice at an old dog.

In *The Magic Mountain* Hans Castorp's evening activities—reading, thinking, dreaming—are described as his "sovereignty." I've always liked that definition. One has to look after the world.

My first two trips: my first independent journey took me to Prague. From my first moments there I was bewitched by its foreignness. Prague smelled different from Krakow; the end of September had brought on autumn's chills, and a stove was burning here and there, stoked by brown coal, not black. I came from a country of black coal. Dusk in Prague was different from dusk in Krakow, the shadows gathered differently. The shop windows were different. The streetcars were another species entirely, they were quicker, their bells rang differently. I got to know foreignness, the foreignness of a language that sounded familiar, but not the same. I fell in love with foreignness; I strolled the streets of old Prague where no one knew me. I was foreign to them too, but I also became a little foreign to myself, and thus a little more real, as if made of slightly sturdier stuff.

Two years later I traveled to Lwow and met foreignness there too. The city in the hills was spattered with Soviet ugliness. I found foreignness in my hometown. I found foreignness within me.

What's great can seldom be expressed.
We're free to tackle smaller matters, though.

My Krakow family belonged almost exclusively to the category of the impoverished intelligentsia (the intelligentsia has grown ever poorer over the last hundred and fifty years; we're lucky that they still exist at all!). My relatives—the kinship was often distant, the blood ties were thin, but this never bothered the members of that family-minded clan—almost always lived in cramped little apartments. It wasn't unusual for three people to be cooped up in two small rooms or even one. A system of folding cots and sofas had to be devised. The apartments radically altered their appearance every evening. You might think you'd stumbled into a hospital, for white sheets had completely transformed the landscape of a room that had just now been a parlor. They covered it in snowdrifts. The next morning these same abodes once more became altars to dailiness, thickly layered in shelves, wardrobes, libraries. Each piece of furniture possessed a different aesthetic pedigree; no one had the time or money to "decorate" the apartment. The furniture there had mostly been salvaged from bygone times, or picked up cheaply from looters. The cupboards were stacked with suitcases or with unshifting strata of preserves. Oil paintings and watercolors, the work of Sunday painters, friends of the family, hung every which way on the walls: some hung straight, while others were perpendicular, or simply followed the laws of gravity. Narrow channels between the furnishings permitted cautious passage from one end of the room to the other, to the Cape of Good Hope from the Strait of Magellan.

These apartments called to mind Italian paintings before the discovery of perspective. There was no room for perspective. Objects bulged, bumped, overflowed as in *trecento* paintings. Chairs could be budged by an inch or two, just barely. The table held a flowered tablecloth, the tablecloth held glasses or cups brimming with straw-colored tea. One of my uncles, a literary scholar, lived in a small apartment with his aging parents for decades. Every day he moved scores of books from the sofa to the floor and back again; otherwise, he wouldn't have had anywhere to sleep. But no one even noticed—they had no perspective. It was considered routine, obvious. No one ever mentioned it. Western movies, with their enormous living quarters, came as a shock to us (unless of course they were Italian neorealist films with poor heroes). It was difficult to accept such squandered space from our nonexistent perspective. Children lived with their parents for ages, young married couples lived with their parents, that is, with old married couples, grandsons and grandparents were cheek by jowl. Washers in bathrooms, wardrobes full of pickles, bicycles in the bedroom, baby buggies chained to banisters in stairwells.

Nothing got thrown out. If someone managed to get a new refrigerator—it did happen now and then—he held on to the old one just in case. Sometimes a balcony might hold an archaic, useless icebox, black with age, the kind that required sky-blue blocks of ice hewn perhaps from Alpine glaciers, and standing by its side would be a defunct Soviet freezer that had already uttered its last wheeze. Those who'd survived Siberia or the German camps were especially tenacious; they clung to everything, bread crusts, empty jam jars, every scrap of packaging, wrapping paper, string, everything. But it wasn't just camp veterans who hoarded useless things: it was an unspoken rule. If you bought a new iron, you kept the old one even if using it meant setting the house ablaze. When you got a new radio, you didn't toss the old one out. So all these old objects stayed huddled on balconies, in hallways and pantries, as if they held the hidden possibility that life might someday start moving backward, not forward according to time's inexorable laws. And then these corpses of objects—rusty bikes, ruptured typewriters, broken sewing machines, parched fountain pens, coffee grinders with missing cranks—would suddenly become indispensable, would come to life, begin to rattle, moan, turn, type, sew, whirl, and then follow us backward like faithful dogs. But this was an understandable reaction to Utopia, to a corrupt, ersatz Utopia falsely promising a joyous, radiant future, a safe port in the storm. Oh, fine, sure, great, Krakow's inhabitants seemed to say, we know, a marvelous future is on its way, but we've got our doubts, and since we barely scrape by in our ordinary lives of Mondays, Tuesdays, Wednesdays, and Thursdays, not to mention Sundays, we'll go back to the past just in case, and keep on piling up old stuff. Maybe you can't turn back the clock, but that still seems more practical and doable than your Utopia, since life just keeps getting harder and further away from that preordained paradise. Your Utopia isn't coming, but perhaps there was a Golden Age in times gone by and we may be able to draw nearer by scaling our pyramid of dead objects as if it were a lookout tower in the woods.

What a contrast! The young poet earnestly prepares himself for his future work by reading the great poets of his own and other languages. He comes to know poetry's splendid past; he reads about those moments when inspiration's flame threatened the equilibrium of the sober, daily world, when poets made the laws that others followed. He studies the epics that captured those ardent moments. He himself undergoes moments of revelation and boldly hopes that he too will one day be worthy of standing alongside the ancient poets.

After a while he gradually begins to take part in the literary life of his own nation; he gives readings, meets others who, like him, have just begun to write and publish. He makes friends with some of them. Nonetheless what a shock, what distress when compared to the glorious past! The readings are attended by some fifteen, or maybe only eight, people. It's not just the pathetic attendance; if the fifteen (or eight) people constituted a choice selection of the absent community at large, that would be one thing. But an old lady in the first row, a basket case in the second, and a lone teenager in the back don't strike him as an appropriate delegation from the particular city that he and his fellow poets have chosen to visit. And even some of the writers he's gotten to know (and they're legion, as if they'd been dunked in some peculiar horn of plenty—scarcely any readers but swarms of writers!) are hardly awe-inspiring. There are even mock-demons among them, whose narrow, foxy faces demonstrate only two things, an appetite for life, and a growing disillusionment, even humiliation: the endless quest for fellowships, the perpetual finagling of invitations to festivals where they'll pick up some pocket money plus a couple of days' room and board. They too probably possess some five minutes' worth of poetry, at least when no one's there to see them, but when they're with others, what comes out isn't poetry but the journeyman's small-scale yearning, the bitterness of unrealized dreams, the poor man's greed and cunning, the envy of the thwarted suitor.

Such a contrast. There—grandeur, clouds, thunderbolts, sublimity. Here—endless discussions of authors' rights, grant applications, plotting, squabbles, poverty.

At first perhaps too much solitude, too many ecstatic revelations, but after that, in the later, lesser career, not enough of either. As if God and the world couldn't get on together (but did they ever?).

Every time I went back to Krakow I restaged the same scene: leaving home. In Krakow I didn't always get enough to eat, I often froze at Mrs. C.'s underheated place. So returning to Gliwice seemed like reaching a safe haven, going home. To leave our warm house on a Sunday evening wasn't easy; it took a certain effort, especially during winter, with snow falling. You had to get to the station and wait for the train, which was rarely on time. Then finally you'd reach Krakow late at night, with no one to meet you, and the infrequent streetcars would clang their bells aggressively at truant pedestrians. It wasn't easy.

My parents were good to me, they took me in joyfully each time, and I was glad to see them, too, but I wasn't especially sorry to go. Home was too tame, too safe. Leaving home meant abandoning routine for the unknown, for quests and adventures. As I trudged to the station through the snow, I felt almost like Amundsen setting out for the South Pole. Your heart aches when you leave—but you also anticipate the pleasures and discoveries that await you in the great, wide world.

Exiles' lamentations should be taken with a grain of salt—unless, of course, the émigrés in question were forced out with bayonets. But as a rule we shouldn't take their mournful sighs too much to heart, since what drove them from their homes was curiosity. And they are authentically sad afterward, since real, ardent curiosity can never truly be sated. But most of us who live in strange cities and foreign nations left home willingly, seeking the thrill of novelty. We look back heartsick with longing—for nothing is simple and unambiguous—but we also gaze yearningly toward the future, the poles, the North Star, the Southern Cross.

One word had a magical meaning for me. It came up now and then in philosophy classes (you never bumped into it during psychology lectures!). I learned to comprehend its sense only slowly, gradually, but it held a piercing truth that touched me long before I grasped its meaning. Not many words provide us with a moment of pure bliss. But this word gave me the kind of sudden joy that an amnesiac must experience on unexpectedly recovering the name of his dearest friend. This was the word "whole." It's often misused by slipshod thinkers. But it's fallen out of fashion generally; at best it's uttered elegiacally, as a one-word obituary for something we've lost and can never recover, something that once enveloped us without our even realizing what a kingly honor we'd received.

The way I experienced the word had nothing to do with the lecturer's intent; he could praise it, mock it, or mourn it, it made no difference. I understood just enough to imagine what it might be like to belong consciously to a "whole," what it would mean to know that I wasn't alone, wasn't just an atom whirling through cold space beneath the lens of some scientific instrument, wasn't simply a scrap, a microscopic speck mysteriously endowed with reason, introspection, sex, and intellect. For there existed, right at hand, a rich, full wholeness of life, to which I belonged, along with others like me, a whole that I might someday grasp by way of thought or the written page, though I knew that I'd never get all of it. (And so much the better! Why would I wish to exhaust such a substance?) And even if I never reached it, it wouldn't mean that it isn't there. It is, it endures, it imperceptibly shapes my existence, and not just mine alone. I have access to this whole even when I'm not thinking or writing about it, simply because I'm a living person, I belong to the commonwealth of the living, and each of us has access to it, through our bodies, through our breath, through our minds, our imaginations; you only need to trust yourself, and to believe that it, the whole, exists. You can approach it only if you believe in its existence; otherwise this makes about as much sense as moving closer to a painting in a museum when you don't acknowledge the worth of art.

I got drunk on the thought of a whole awaiting me and everyone who sought it. But my teachers spoke, by and large, as though it didn't exist. It did exist at one time, or so it's commonly thought. But it crumbled long ago, fell into thousands of pieces, like a Chinese porcelain vase. The prying pettiness of science, the modern artist's irony, and, worst of all, the shocking cruelty of recent history—all joined forces to shatter it. There is no whole and never will be, all we've got are tiny totalities and their mock high priests, the specialists, specialists on the first decade of the fourteenth century or the Elizabethan sonnet, on the fourth chromosome or hypertension. So we live on, but as tenants of an outsized orphanage, a cosmic trash bin.

"Surely you all know *Bouvard and Pécuchet*, Flaubert's final, unfinished novel?" our professor asked. "No? Then you've got to read it. Flaubert couldn't finish it, you see, because one can complete only those works firmly grounded on some concept of the whole. Flaubert died in 1880 while working on the manuscript of that marvelous, dreary, comic, hopeless failure of a book, that inventory detailing the manifold impotence of human knowledge and imagination. He died because he couldn't finish it! Yes, I'll risk a diagnosis. Cause of death: uncompletable novel. Not syphilis or a stroke, an unfinished manuscript. It couldn't be done, for all the author's brisk confidence: in his final letters he announces that he'll wrap things up, then move on to a new book about Thermopylae! I hope the doctors concur with my postmortem. Please bear in mind, 1880, the last decade of Friedrich Nietzsche's conscious life, the railroad covers the entire continent of Europe, the twentieth century comes closer, the century of unfinished writings. No one in this century ever died of an unfinished novel." (It goes without saying that I got the book from the library the next day and laughed my way through the adventures of those imbecilic copyists.)

But my encounters with this wholeness weren't limited to lectures. I sometimes experienced a similar feeling while walking through the center of Krakow. The narrow medieval streets leading to the Old Market, the shifting perspectives, the nervous rhythm of the rooftops—all joined to form the blood vessels of a living, organic system. You could circle the old city center by way of the Planty gardens in an hour or less. Church steeples, white or blood-red, pierced the vast canopies of chestnuts, maples, ashes; they towered above the foliage like grownups hovering watchfully over their young in family photographs. I didn't think about it every day, it didn't always occur to me. Days and weeks went by when my mind was taken up by completely mundane matters: will I get credit for history of philosophy, have I got enough money for both concerts and lunches, does my girlfriend still remember me? But sometimes, at odd moments, it seemed to me that I perceived the city's unity, that I grasped it by means of a special sense, the sense of wholeness.

The medieval city offered a ready model of the cosmos, it had everything: the river, the meadows, the houses and trees, the churches and cloister gardens, the fortified walls enclosing the city and the gates that opened it, like the valves of a human heart, in an ageless rhythm of day and night, sleep and waking, sloth and the merchant's sly hyperactivity. And this was the center to which the needles of all the compasses drifted, whether consciously or not; each apartment house took its cue from the center; you could gauge the distance to the Old Market from any point in the city by way of something like an unseen Geiger counter. The Old Market was the city's magnetic pole, its destiny, its boundary, its pride. And even the city's ramshackle outskirts, a no-man's-land overgrown with weeds, where old automobiles and empty cans sunk in stoic ataraxia slowly but surely succumbed to rust, even these peripheries sensed dimly that they weren't entirely on their own, autonomous, dere-lict; they were the city's skin, a self-renewing epidermis linked by elongated nerves to its omnipotent center. The sun and moon were likewise city property, they circled it faithfully in winter and summer alike, at times pale and weary, veiled by mist and lacy clouds, or just the opposite, shining briskly, joyfully, triumphantly.

It was a matter of pride to belong to such a city, to be a piece of it, striding its streets like a farmer measuring his fields. I was just a student who went home to Gliwice every couple of weeks, I wasn't even registered to live in Krakow, but perhaps I felt its radiance, its ancient power all the more strongly for that. Not always, though: at times I doubted Krakow's majesty, hence doubted the very possibility of a tangible, magical wholeness in our day and age (as if the city really had become my model of the world!). I laughed at myself sometimes, at my comic exaltation, my excess. The city lived on, but the Vistula River was filthy, almost black. I adored the medieval walls, the Renaissance spires, but I refused to see the secret police cars, I chose not to recognize that my lovely (at moments!) city was governed by idiots, tinpot Communists who took their orders from Warsaw, from Moscow. It was the uncouth, provincial outpost of a Soviet colony, a caricature of "wholeness," not a true locus of life-giving energy.

Did I really not realize this, hadn't they drummed it into me (not through terror but with the tired smile of a bully who's had enough and would rather act like what is called a decent fellow)? Hadn't they forced me to pore over philosophy and psychology texts translated not so much from the Russian as from the Soviet? I knew—but at times I wanted to forget. And didn't I know that Krakow bore an open wound, an empty quarter holding not ruins but ramshackle huts, old houses even more decayed than those in other districts? (Neglect was the norm under the Communists.) This was the graveyard quarter—Kazimierz, the district of the Jews, who were gone now, who'd been first driven out by the Nazis, forced to live on the far side of the river, and then systematically murdered. Didn't I know that no city on earth could recover from such a tragedy, regardless of whether it tried to forget or struggled

to understand the past and pay homage to its victims? Didn't I realize that the twenty years lying between me and the slaughter were
next to nothing? That moans and whispers must still sound in many
tongues—in Yiddish, in Hebrew, in Polish and German, in the language of inhuman pain—throughout a seemingly medieval town
that was also a phonograph record? I loved to contemplate the
nature of memory and to summon up earlier times; how could I
possibly neglect the suffering that lay so close at hand?

I knew, I thought about it: Kazimierz was part of my circuit, it
took its place in the terrain that shaped my strolls. It was a different
space, empty and mute, an island almost at the city's heart, a
deserted wasteland; in the sixties it was peopled chiefly by mindless
drunks and raucous hookers. It was the district of walls thick with
dust and ashes between which gaunt, anemic willows sprouted. The
district of the old cemetery that went almost unvisited back then.
An empty district, with unkempt, uncared-for houses, where only
nettles and enormous burdocks flourished. And I knew that those
vanished Jews had been—potentially—my kin, myself, the same as
me. I tried not to idealize them, I knew that, just as in any group of
people, I'd have made friends with only a few of them—but this was
precisely the measure of their humanness, the imperfection and
frailty that I shared so perfectly with them.

I knew, I remembered; kind spirits had somehow sewn into my
skin an aversion to the anti-Semitism I sometimes encountered
among my fellow students or even my teachers, beginning with my
National Democrat grandmother, my mother's mother, whom I
couldn't bear; I've never forgiven her shameful behavior (her abuse
was exclusively verbal, but it was as relentless and resonant as
drumbeats).

I knew about both of them, the wound of Kazimierz and the
wound of Soviet totalitarianism. But there were moments when I
forgot what I knew, when I preferred to place my faith not in what I

knew but in what I felt, saw, and heard, when I chose to note only the city's countless slivers of reality, since the word "whole" did exist in spite of all, and did give me moments of joy (or sorrow). Not just the word—the shiver of wholeness wouldn't desist even when reason categorically refused to acknowledge its existence. I knew of both wounds, and I was inclined in theory to dispense with all illusions: the world is unfinished, in tatters, frayed like a second-hand shirt, and not even a medieval miracle could heal its infectious ailment. So spoke reason, and I earnestly seconded its claim. But the naïve force of small epiphanies still hounded me; they lay in wait for me and other wanderers throughout the city. Even my walks through the outskirts of Kazimierz, where Jewish civilization came face-to-face with Catholicism's salient sentinels in the shape, say, of the ornate Church of Corpus Christi, whose dark nave was lazily traversed by a shaft of sunlight bearing careless, dancing specks of dust—even these walks were not entirely free of the rapture I struggled to contain.

There was something amoral, shameless in the inertia of existence, the inertia that permitted even formerly Jewish houses, some of them reaching back to the seventeenth or eighteenth century, to betray the memory of their inhabitants if only by uncritically entertaining, as always, the light and the rain, the day, the endless evenings of June, the scents of tempting autumn. There was something mysterious in the way that the earth and things existed, avidly and intensively. They seized each moment, exploited every opportunity, if only to enjoy, in a lazy, catlike way, the July heat or even November's drizzling rain, the crackling dry frost of a February night. They cynically agreed to every minute of the year, every change in the season or the weather, if only they could keep on being. Anything is better than the nothingness that so preoccupies the modern philosophers. No, the earth and things had no use for nothingness; their interests lay with clouds and rain, the enthralling progress of nights and days.

Steel bridges stretched blissfully each time the temperature rose, wooden balconies creaked gently, as if to say, "You, people, keep right on murdering one another, but you'll have to forgive us for staying on the sidelines, for steering clear of those ever-changing theories to which we pay no heed. Our task is far too serious for us to mind the fickle temper of the times; we, things, are reality's roots, we are the pillars of being. We've got no use for young literary critics with their irony. Long duration is our fate and not the short-lived nuptial flight of fledgling poets. Any insurance agent would understand us better than an au courant philosopher."

Was this the "whole" or simply voices and whispers issuing forth from under reality's hat? Perhaps the "whole" had been shattered once and for all—or so my mind insisted, so my reason argued, so the scholars showed. But experience was more persuasive than reason. It wasn't just my lonely strolls and solitary revelations that led me to this conclusion. It was also other people, the people I loved and those I merely observed. Some of them lived audaciously, as if the "whole" really existed. They staked everything on one card, lived wisely and briskly, taking risks. I sometimes caught a glimpse of genuine life, of verve and strength even in the eyes of the occasional passerby. So people too possessed an implacable, iron will to be, to survive in spite of everything, the same determination I'd discovered in the earth and in things.

At times I seemed to sense a vast rift between the university and life. A spirit of profound skepticism, of doubt in life's worth, enveloped the university. Meanwhile, though, various daredevils persisted in living honest, energetic lives. They paid no heed to professorial preachings, they ignored the outpouring of recent findings in dreary dust jackets, they disregarded the dismal decrees of French philosophers proclaiming (if I recall correctly) that man is dead. Even raising the subject of the "whole" was a bit awkward, since you ended up either among the historians of ideas, who spoke of wholeness only in dry, well-nigh sepulchral tones, or among those specializing in life, who steered scrupulously clear of theoretical speculations, sensing that such idle thought might prove suicidal to them.

I found more skepticism than daring in art as well, more irony, more narcissistic fascination with form than concern for the fittest subject of study: the great, stern, inscrutable world. Poets kept their eyes fixed on poetry, on linguistic riddles. One miracle alone held all their interest: that poetry still managed to exist (as if the world's existence weren't far more miraculous!). The greatest artists of our age—more my grandfather's coevals than my father's—acted as if they wanted to annihilate the forms of art they practiced. Picasso worked to destroy art, Stravinsky went after music, while Joyce's target was the novel. They acted as if history had run its course, as if future generations were doomed, as if they wished to strip them of the joy of painting, writing, composing, thinking. The "whole"— who still wasted breath on wholeness? Who worried about a human community that was perhaps still yearning for a new word?

Wandering through poor, deserted Kazimierz and thinking about reality's many-storied house, rambling through this orphaned district in the autumn dusk, or in the springtime when swallows, spry and lively as tourists scouring a Greek temple, return from sojourns overseas, wandering, mulling questions about future, past, and present—it was, of course, eccentric. Or am I just ascribing to my early self—so much younger than the author of these words that he could easily be my little brother, even my son—the interests and worries that preoccupy me now? I don't think so; it seems to me that the same questions plagued me back then, although perhaps I didn't understand their sense the way I think I do now.

From Kazimierz I set off for St. Catherine's Church; I turned up narrow Skaleczna Street toward the Church on the Rock, glimpsing en route an ancient wall surrounding one of Krakow's many monastic gardens (a fair-sized meadow, given over to sunshine and cats, sprawled beyond the wall); then I walked along the dark, captive Vistula toward Salwator Hill. I crossed the ugly, Austrian part of Wawel Castle beneath Franz Josef's dark brown barracks and passed the student boathouse; the Norbertine convent rose in front of me, with its gentle Tuscan silhouette. Once I reached the convent, I turned right and headed down a path by the Rudawa, steering left of the august hill of Gontyn, Queen Jadwiga Street, and the atelier of the Party sculptors who kept the city stocked with stately bronze Lenins. I hit my favorite path right afterward, and struck out toward the Kosciuszko Mound.

In May and June the grass was the green of fresh, careless foliage; the birch trees flaunted their tiny leaves, each of which was perfect. The green light shaped its own separate space even though the new city was just a few paces away. I could hear the asthmatic wheezing of trucks hauling sand; gigantic cement mixers bearing enormous, revolving white pears leaned heavily against a little hill. I felt the city's breath. If you went just a little bit farther, you could see concrete apartment blocks—the white pears' progeny!—disfiguring the landscape. I didn't look; I chose to gaze instead at the towers of the Cameldolite church at Bielany, which rose above a bronze forest.

The dead were also part of the whole, of course; the armies of the dead and all they'd left behind in music, in art and poetry, in architecture, in mathematics. Sometimes one of Sep-Szarzynski's poems meant more to me than any modern masterpiece. Jan Kochanowski's laments hadn't lost their mournful power. Archilochus's fragments enthralled me with their mixture of shabbiness and sublimity. One Chinese poet—Tu Fu? Li Po?—pierced the curtain time had hung between us with the speed of lightning. The dead hadn't vanished entirely; you had to train your memory to receive as many signals from the past as possible. And not just this; they had to be in usable condition. We write poems while listening to the dead—but we write them for the living.

Even Death itself—that connoisseur of form, that illustrious caesura—had found its place within the whole's elastic frame. It conducted its far-flung conspiracies here by way of its underpaid agents. It killed Mozart in his thirty-sixth year while granting Michelangelo a long life; it borrowed a German soldier's rifle to take aim at Krzysztof Baczynski's brow. You could write and talk freely about Death; it had no recourse to censors forbidding any mention of its name. But you could never be sure what it was you were talking about: Death proper, or what we'd made of it, recasting it in our own image.

One path veered off to one side of Krakow's main promenade. The natives strolled staidly along this promenade whenever the weather permitted; old couples debating the merits of various recipes for plum jam, fathers and frisky children. But the side path skirted a garden that had once belonged to Miroslaw Dzielski and then vanished into little gullies and valleys that couldn't be seen from the main walkway. Here you might happen upon a pensive fox, a weasel frozen in fear, a hare, a black-eyed deer. I don't know why, but virtually no one used this peripheral path—perhaps from fear of loneliness? of chaos? You could get lost here, even though it was really just a tiny mock-up of an authentic wilderness. Every now and then a peasant would work the meadow, his small, gaunt horse pulling the plow with verve (the meadows and scraps of fields must have been too steep for tractors). Swallows swirled in the azure skies and an ancient stork swooped slowly over the Vistula.

Wholeness? What I saw in the earth, in things, in the wintry obstinacy of all those who clung to existence, was linked to life's lower limits, and not to its loftier realms. If the whole had in fact survived, if it hadn't yet yielded to final destruction, it was thanks to the modest, constant energies of endurance, implacable as that little horse working the field. But it lacked a high style, elevated tones, lofty voices holding forth, powerful and persuasive, impervious to sneers. The whole exists only in part, supported by the enormous exertions of humble little creatures serving the cosmos; it might seem that our Atlas, the Atlas for our times, has only calves (insanely powerful calves, as in da Vinci's drawings), but the poor thing's missing a head. And that's why—is that why?—the whole is incomplete. I wouldn't have dared to make such a claim in a philosophy seminar; they would have laughed at me. But no one could object here among the little gullies smelling of June hay, beneath the linden boughs heavy with blossoms and leaves: yes, the whole exists, but no, it's not whole.

Whenever I came back from a long walk the dusk would already be settling in; like a tired old magician it concealed the town's rooftops and spires beneath a cloak of evening mist.

Anyone who composes a defense of poetry in prose neglects the writing of poems in the process. Can you really defend poetry this way?

We found a beautiful little cat, unhappy and abandoned, in the woods of Sèvres outside Paris. He soon became a dear and tender friend, but he died two months later of an illness that even the veterinarian couldn't diagnose. He wouldn't eat anything. He died very peacefully, as if lost in thought, worrying about one thing only: loneliness. He turned his back on me and looked the other way. He didn't want to meet my eyes.

———

For a long time scholars apparently refused to see Ovid's late poetry, written in exile, as even worth comparing to the earlier work, chiefly the *Metamorphoses*. They didn't like the tone of the later cycles (*Tristia* and *Epistulae ex Ponto*), their air of loss and lamentation.

It is a well-known fact that scholars are often hard-of-hearing. We must note in passing how vastly our own century differs from the times of Augustus. Ovid was forced to abandon Rome, the capital of the world, for a small, squalid town on the empire's outskirts in what is now Romania, a frontier town under constant attack by the barbarians. Modern Romanian exiles now exchange Tomi for Paris. But the poems Ovid wrote in Tomi forge a perfect alloy of grief, despair, humiliation, arrogance, wit, self-mockery, and self-pity. Ovid is talking to Caesar, not God. All the same, he speaks in the splendid language of Job, Job who had the misfortune of being witty on top of everything else.

There's no such thing as progress in literature, but there's no dearth of shifts and displacements. Today's Jobs—Ovid showed them the way—are uncommonly witty. If they were any funnier, they'd have to join the circus, or even write for sitcoms.

What links poetry and music? Poetry.

The imagination's ceaseless quarrel with the world: whenever the imagination grows too strong, it is cut down to size by the mocking laughter of cocksure realists, tax collectors, and successful businessmen (to say nothing of strict moralists like Pascal or Simone Weil). But every time the sober world regains the upper hand so completely that the imagination lies near death, a distant province gives birth to some poet who will write a new poem one day.

Camus's *First Man* (a splendid book) is a tribute to silence, in this case to the silence of a poor, simple, largely illiterate family. Anyone who speaks, who does business with expression, betrays existence; existence is silent and complete, ineffable, and any utterance can only diminish it. But there really isn't any choice, especially for a writer. We have to break the silence, however painfully, and thus betray the very substance of which we speak (there is no other). And Camus, like any writer, is guilty of this betrayal. It seems as though he found a certain space for himself, a buffer zone between silence and speech: the Mediterranean's dry landscapes, beaches at dawn and dusk, spiked grass, sallow palms, the streets of Algiers (the same city in which Cervantes spent several years as a captive of the Barbary pirates), unpeopled by the ferocious heat. Mediterranean dryness has this distinction: it borders on both copper and the deep blue, living, swaying sea. Nothing can be said about the sea, only the beach is eloquent.

Childhood illnesses: fever, parched lips, and the taste of cool tea with lemon.

Gombrowicz's books were hard to come by. He wasn't banned as strictly as other émigré writers. In the period around October 1956, *Ferdydurke* and *Bakakaj* turned up in domestic editions. Of course, they vanished in an instant, and when I was a student, no one even dreamed of finding them in ordinary bookstores. Like the old Art Nouveau editions of Nietzsche, Gombrowicz had to be tracked down in secondhand bookshops. I remember how one of the booksellers greeted me when I asked if he happened to have any Gombrowicz. This was in one of the secondhand book-stores near the Old Market: a narrow, sparsely lit shop and a long table strewn with books, the sedate smell of dust. The owner of the bookshop—one of a handful of booksellers who'd managed to survive the nationalization of trade—was an old man dressed in black (or so I see him in memory, but his age may have been more a product of my youthful optics than an empirical fact).

Besides the worthy bookseller, the shop also held a solitary lady, clearly a friend of the owner. So I asked if he had any Gombrowicz. Instead of just giving the usual answer, the bookseller set sail on a torrent of speech.

"Young man," he said after he'd taken a moment to look me over and had obviously reached the conclusion that he wasn't up against an agent of the secret police or the ministry of finance, that I was just an ordinary student, most likely from an educated family, in short, one of his own, "young man, I'm not sure you're acting wisely in reading or even wanting to read Witold Gombrowicz. I'm not at all sure. We live, after all, in very unhappy times. Trying times. I'm sure that you don't need convincing on that score. And meanwhile, who is this Witold Gombrowicz? A joker. Not a serious writer, not a patriot. A joker, cocky, maybe even clever. Not without talent. Oh no, you couldn't ever say he lacked for talent. But unfortunately he took the cynic's route. And that isn't what we need in our present situation. He's not the writer for us. It worries me, young people's interest in Gombrowicz; you're not the first student to come asking about his books. You young people would be better off reading more serious authors—why aren't you looking for Golubiew or Malewska?"

(I got to know Hanna Malewska much later; I used to stop by at her tiny apartment near Freedom Square.)

"And by the way," the bookseller concluded, "I haven't got any Gombrowicz in stock right now. Come by another time." His companion said nothing, but I sensed their solidarity.

I said goodbye and left the dark bookshop.

I liked the bookseller, even though I didn't share his views on Gombrowicz. He spoke calmly, he wasn't a caricature, a cliché. I couldn't agree with him, but it struck me that I'd just come across a living specimen of the nineteenth-century Polish patriot; all he needed was the cloak.

I didn't agree with him, he amused me. What did my country need? It's not an easy job, figuring out what a country needs. Gombrowicz liked playing the fool—so in that sense the bookseller was right. But literature sometimes plays tricks on its readers and even its authors; in spite of all Gombrowicz's theoretical programs and pronouncements, true seriousness, the vibrant gravity of his life, did make its way into his writing.

Linguistic definitions of poetry, and of literature generally, predominate in our age. This means that in defining literature—incidentally, why do we need to define literature, anyway? who bothers to define rain?—the first move is sticking out your tongue. This approach links thinkers as diverse as the structuralists, on the one hand, and Joseph Brodsky, on the other, a great poet closer to metaphysics than to science.

It's a tricky problem, and an immensely important question. If literature were nothing more than its linguistic material, then it would be only a refined amusement for educated people, something along the lines of crossword puzzles for the elite. It must be admitted that a fair number of so-called literary works don't go much beyond this, though they don't lack for enthusiastic readers (the creators of crossword puzzles also can't complain about their popularity, or so it seems to me).

In his marvelous book on Saint Augustine, Peter Brown says: "In deciding for a 'life in philosophy' Augustine didn't renounce a barren culture rooted in literature. Just the opposite—he worked to battle an equally powerful and self-conscious late Roman way of life." Let's keep in mind this one phrase, "a barren culture rooted in literature." The late Roman context is clearly important here, but we also glimpse a broader truth in Brown's comment: any culture based solely on language, and on literature conceived as a linguistic exercise, as rhetoric, must finally grow dry. Like philosophy, literature must keep asking itself the ultimate questions. Otherwise it becomes mere literature! (And philosophy will be mere philosophy . . .)

Literature occupies a highly ambiguous position. It is—at least potentially—the queen of culture, a grande dame, a transforming experience, a shock, a revelation. But it falls from these heights with the greatest of ease to become pure gamesmanship, a conundrum, a showcase for linguistic sleight of hand. Sometimes in even a great poet's work you may stumble across a sudden drop into mere language, rhetoric, even idle chatter.

A warm day, a light rain; the poetry of Robert Desnos.

It would be a mistake to conclude that the Krakow I knew was peopled exclusively by beings from a different geological era, meek and quiet, waiting to be placed in a museum. After all, there was Professor U.

Unlike Professors Leszczynski and Szuman, Professor U. was a man of the moment, hence the moment's master. He fit the age so perfectly that it was surprising that he could even be perceived against its backdrop. He was delighted with the historical moment that fate had granted him; it might seem that Communism had been dreamed up just for him. It was for his sake that Marx had slaved away in the Reading Room of the British Museum; and Engels had ruined his eyes for Professor U. It was because of him that Lenin and Stalin—in compliance with the celebrated Eleventh Thesis—hadn't stopped at simply understanding the world, and had seen fit to change it. The bourgeoisie and landed gentry were shot for his benefit, the peasants were starved, the intellectuals murdered. And the playing rules were relaxed in '56 so that he'd have no problem hanging on to his holdings, and thus no need to tremble with fear. All this so that Professor U. might rejoice in his villa and garden, his directorship, his flashy neckties, his trips to the West, his obedience. The great revolutionaries' struggles hadn't been in vain. He had to restrain his jubilance, conceal his bliss—not everyone grasped history's logic, not everyone was free from petty jealousy. He wanted to leap with glee like a preschooler, to warble triumphal arias, take encores like Caruso. But no, things had turned out differently, he was forced to suppress his excitement; his voice was profoundly pragmatic and only an unusually musical ear could catch the hints of a hidden euphoria.

Professor U. was also the chairman of the Krakow Society of Atheists and Freethinkers. You had to be truly contemptible to do battle with the Church in a state committed to religion's abolition; but our professor was more than equal to the task. He became the city's leading atheist, the atheists' local bishop. Was it from conviction? I don't think he had any convictions, he was simply a perfect example of someone who shared his era's views without reservation.

He'd become a university professor by chance; he might just as easily have been a dairy plant director, the commander of a regiment of sappers. Professional training was beside the point; obedience and energy came first. His energy was obvious; his obedience was easy to imagine. Anyone who managed simultaneously to chair the atheists' committee, work at the university, and—another job I haven't mentioned yet—speak at various functions in his capacity as "Party committee lecturer" was more than just obedient. He competed eagerly for the privilege of representing the powers that be. Obedience involves commands and punishments, but this was a matter of incentives and rewards. So Professor U. was very busy, rushing from one meeting to the next, even canceling his classes on occasion. Sometimes it seemed that he hadn't turned up in weeks—the bulletin then announced that Professor U. was ill. When he returned to class a month later, he didn't resemble a wan convalescent in the least. Just the opposite—he was tan, like a man who'd just spent a vacation in the Alps. No one dared to check.

First and foremost, though, there was his energetic aplomb: U., who ended up a professor the same way that someone might become the boss's son-in-law (he'd married the Party), loved to flaunt his (highly doubtful) expertise. I don't recall a single original thought, a single memorable comment ever leaving his lips (even though as a young man he'd published a good book on gestalt). He was exceptionally lucid. I am here, in this moment, I'm actively present at this very minute, he seemed to say. I don't daydream, I don't put off for tomorrow, I don't look forward, I don't look back—and I don't understand those romantic poets for whom the present day wasn't enough, who were always sighing after bygone times or yearning for the future. Unlike them, I am thoroughly contented with the present, I imagine nothing, aspire to nothing, I've already achieved it all.

He had a high forehead and a bishop's large nose. He was a man of the moment.

Just listening to music carefully! Music is uncommonly tolerant; it gives us access to ourselves even when our minds are elsewhere, in a commuter train, while reading or writing, when we're chatting with others or buying a shirt. An unscrupulous adman can use a bit of Mozart's *Requiem*, one of the greatest works our forebears have bequeathed us, to hawk his client's product on TV. It's possible to understand the Polish refugees in September 1939 who paid gold for some bread and a cup of milk. But how can you comprehend a businessman who squanders Mozart's gold in a time of peace and prosperity—and for nothing? Listening to music carefully—it rarely seems to happen—would open a kingdom of untold riches before us, an incomparably fecund realm. It's the same with poetry. If someone were born who really knew how to read poems (the rare poems that merit such a reading), who read them better than their own authors, who knew how to concentrate splendidly, not, like Eastern wise men, on the void, but on the whole, what unimaginable results might be achieved?

A person who says (as if summing up his life): as a young man I liked Mahler's Fifth Symphony the best, but the Ninth's my favorite now.

A day when our writer was preoccupied with cleaning his three fountain pens. I've never seen a crow spend a whole day preening its feathers (or a cat spend more than half an hour on its fur).

What poverty, to write, and then assign the writing either a plus or a minus for morality (a proclivity of our times). As if it weren't enough to write and trust the writing to bring forth truth from its own substance; no faith in one's self.

Good and evil don't reside in plus or minus signs, in commentaries, in the tendency that guides a given book. They lie in the manner of speaking (which the writer himself can never quite hear, since we don't know our own selves).

B. said to me, you know, I'm not fit for anything, I've got no way to make a living, the only thing I can come up with is "lectures on silence for young ladies."

When it comes to punctuation, the period is the haughtiest of signs. After me the deluge . . .

Two young poets publish a book, in which they insist that their country has not yet been described (giving their readers to understand that other countries and continents have done better in this regard).

But the world has never been described anywhere! There isn't any country whose reality has been described! Reality mocks description.

In 362 Julian the Apostate issued an edict (intended for Christians) which proclaimed that only those professors believing in the Greek gods would henceforth be permitted to teach Homer, Hesiod, Demosthenes, Herodotus, Thucydides, Isocrates, and Lysias. If this principle were universally applied, the educational systems of all countries would collapse, regardless of their ideologies.

I often went to the Philharmonic and more than once heard works from the classical canon for the first time; in Gliwice the only musical institution was the operetta located on the city's outskirts, near the so-called Bird District. It was called the Bird District because all the streets in that neighborhood took their names from songbirds. And in truth the blackbirds and orioles, the thrushes and nightingales that sang so rapturously in its gardens were far superior to the operatic ingenues with cheeks daubed with rosy powder. The birds dominated this competition all the more readily since they were generally invisible, concealed in a thicket of branches and leaves; they made their presence known solely through their song, as if their voices were hiding by themselves among the trees. But who ever listens to birds, who has the time and patience to stand stock-still before a garden throbbing with a blackbird's vernal song? Whereas the princess of the czardas was all too obvious, smeared with pink powder and fluttering her five petticoats. She was too busy taking encore after encore to stay tucked away within a slim poplar's leaves.

The Krakow Philharmonic was another thing entirely; here one might run across the haughty Penderecki. The students of Krakow's music schools turned out in force. Partly cynical and partly eager, they resembled young clerics who meet Saturday evenings outside the church but don't dare display their faith too fervently, and so titter weakly at feeble, off-color jokes. But if it turned out that the visiting virtuoso was to play an unannounced encore, the terror-stricken music students scurried to identify the work. The public at large might get by with ignorance, but it wouldn't do for them, future professionals, not to recognize the piece. You could catch the agitated whispers—"A Brahms sonata," "No, Schubert, F minor," "No, it's Beethoven, opus 31"—that fluttered like dragonflies above the rows of seats. "But I'm telling you, it's Schumann." The music professors kept mum, pretending that they already had all the answers, and couldn't be bothered with such games.

Newcomers also turned up at these concerts, novices with no clue about musical etiquette. And these rank beginners generally committed catastrophic, unforgivable faux pas: they didn't hold their bravos until the piece was over, but greeted the close of the first movement with profligate applause. Perhaps they hoped this ardor would help grease their way into the ranks of the regulars. They couldn't have judged worse! The true connoisseurs were in agony, they'd been torn from their total absorption—or their boredom. They turned ostentatiously, rose from their seats, and cursed the perpetrators with silent stares. But the guilty parties had only the best intentions and didn't understand the reasons for the others' wrath. The musicians, with the tailcoated conductor at their head, didn't like the early bravos either. Some smiled ironically, even scornfully, while others froze into a kind of tableau vivant, pretending that nothing had happened and doing their best to sit out the unwelcome, amateur applause.

This premature applause, this abortive admiration, disrupted the fixed transience of the work; it introduced partisan factions into a composition whose individual movements were meant to stand alongside one another throughout eternity without ever touching, like the columns of a Greek temple. Arthur Honegger's *Liturgical* Symphony, for example, comprises three movements: the *Dies irae: Allegro marcato, De profundis clamavi: Adagio,* and *Dona nobis pacem:*

Andante. The inexperienced enthusiasts rewarded the allegro with their rapture. But their crime met with damning stares, and a wave of dry *sh-sh-sh*'s shook the electrified air, so they didn't dare repeat their gaffe after the lovely *adagio.* The symphony's middle movement was perhaps ill served as a result.

But was their reaction so gauche? Could these ignorant amateurs possibly be right? Was their response perhaps more human, less arrogant than the custom upheld at concert halls throughout the world? When I like something, I clap, I don't wait for the final chords of the sonata or symphony. Why not react right off, from the depths of your soul (if it exists)? Why hold out for another half hour, biting your lips, clenching your hands, perching rapture on erudition's pedestal?

These concerts, with their public made up of the haughty Penderecki, some fledgling musicians, a few impoverished counts, the occasional beauty lost among lovestruck boys staring as if she were the Virgin Mary, and of course some official from the district Party committee, did not immediately reveal music to me in its purest, most passionate form. The Philharmonic at times called to mind the parish church in a thriving mountain village. Penderecki entered amid a flurry of whispers, whispers besieged the beautiful girl who flapped her concert program like a Chinese fan. A plump professor from the Academy of Fine Arts acknowledged his bowing students. A well-known gynecologist accompanied his towering wife, who was supposed to have run off once with an Italian journalist, only to come back a month later. A certain wealthy shoemaker came to the Philharmonic in order to purge himself of the persistent smell of calfskin and oxhide. A thin-lipped philosopher, who was known to dislike art generally but felt nonetheless that everything extant merits due consideration, took his place in the last row. Four nuns, holding hands like preschoolers, smiled happily through both thrillingly tragic works and cheerful pieces, like parts of Stravinsky's *Petrouchka*. But perhaps that's as it should be: I read somewhere that sailors sing sad songs only when they're happy.

Once one of the orchestra members fainted. A very strange affair. The concert broke off and confusion reigned momentarily. It made a tremendous impression on me: fainting onstage is like falling from an airplane, slipping from a different kind of time. I wrote a poem about this extraordinary event, about someone slipping out of music's timelessness. By chance this poem became my poetic debut.

But sometimes—often enough—I forgot the silly, snobbish side of those Philharmonic affairs, and the music's power quelled my doubts. The sense of sight, which compels us to survey our neighbors disdainfully (forgetting, of course, that they're busy doing the same), would vanish, dissipate. It was there, at the Krakow Philharmonic, that I first heard Mozart's wild, rapacious Requiem, which wouldn't let me sleep later that night, and Brahms's Third Symphony, with the piercing, swaying third movement that bears the exceedingly modest name Poco allegretto. I listened to Chopin's ballades, to his nocturnes and mazurkas, all spun, it seemed, from the simplest of songs, from vacation souvenirs and white goose quills. When I'd yielded at last to the music's exaltation, I thought, felt, that music is the world's empress: a regent (for the king has embarked on a long voyage) imposing her own principles and habits, which look arbitrary at first but soon come to seem completely legitimate and necessary. And I sensed, too, that I wasn't the only one undergoing the shift from sardonic observation of the concert hall's occupants to rapt absorption. My experience was no different from that of the other listeners. Almost all of us were entranced, we fell beneath the sway of that unseen regent, stern, yet receptive to our efforts. The slim conductor held his baton by her dispensation, it was she who condoned the pianist's rhythmic sway-

ing—which struck me initially as slightly comical—over the keys of
the black Steinway.

And while this transformation was taking place, I thought that
the great things, like music, generally take one of two shapes. At
times they're insubstantial, frivolous, open to ridicule. Once they
ripen and draw closer to their essence, though, they turn solid, true,
sublime—and this is how we should experience them.

Music puts forth form and rhythm, it builds its airy structures
on a substance as delicate as breath, as time. Music enthralled me,
even though I couldn't play a single instrument, couldn't even hum
the simplest melody on key. I don't have a good ear, not to mention
perfect pitch, which I can only dream of. That is, I have an ear of
sorts, but it's purely internal, it shows itself only passively, in recog-
nizing individual works, in a passive musical memory and an active
enthusiasm that produces no actual results. I even whistle badly. My
musician's ear keeps undercover, like a conspirator who fears the
daylight. Nothing comes to the surface. Hidden deep within my
skull's recesses, it permits only visits from great composers and per-
formers. It's timid, inhibited by its passivity, its faults and imperfections. But when it's seized and completed by the music that it loves,
it vibrates powerfully and sets in motion other inner senses less
crippled than itself.

Another of my aunts, whose husband was a classical philologist—
and an anticlerical agnostic—lived right by St. Florian's Church on
Warsaw Street. Here is what Michal Rozek's guidebook has to say
about the shrine: "Legend links the building of the church to a reliquary of the martyred Saint Florian that had been brought to
Poland. According to tradition, the oxen bearing the saint's remains
stopped on this spot and refused to move until the decision was

made to erect a shrine dedicated to the martyr. The chroniclers tell us that the saint's remains were brought to Poland in 1184 by Prince Kazimierz the Just, who received the reliquary from Pope Lucius II."

My aunt was a pious woman; and St. Florian's engaging, intelligent young priest soon came to her attention. Naturally enough, she invited the young priest to supper. In time he became a family friend. The professor's agnosticism provoked, intrigued, perhaps even inspired him; their dinners frequently turned into heated debates about the existence of God. The discussions must have given the two men pleasure; after all, the young priest didn't really fear for his faith in his tussles with a classical philologist (watch out, though! Classical philologists can be extremely hazardous; each one contains a latent Friedrich Nietzsche). But my uncle certainly enjoyed the company of the young priest, who possessed great charm. He was one of those clerics who manage to unite faith and even discipline with inner freedom, with a free man's sovereignty.

I suspect that my aunt may have been a little jealous; the young priest gave so much thought to his talks with an agnostic! She was the one who'd sought out this charming guest, and there he was, caught up in conversation with his ideological enemy, neglecting his friends for his foes. He didn't ignore her entirely, he always asked about the children, their three children, of whom he'd grown fond. But he clearly cherished his debates with the classical philologist.

At home they called my uncle "the Sword," and he really was fearless. He wasn't a rank-and-file agnostic, not a petty mercenary like Professor U., a militant unbeliever in the service of the state. He was a skeptic, unconvinced, mistrustful of the Church (though he returned to the Church somewhat later, so the young priest finally won the battle in progress at that dark apartment just off

Warsaw Street). But none of this kept him from singing Christmas carols with the young priest! He may have spoken of Auschwitz in their debates, since it lay just an hour and a half away by car: where was God then, while the ovens of Auschwitz flamed? My uncle's family came from those parts, his father had repaired machinery in one of the mines near Auschwitz, so my uncle may have discovered something about the transports to the camp firsthand, or from conversations at home, and not simply from articles in the postwar press, from memoirs, survivors' accounts.

Or perhaps his knowledge of ancient Greece, his passion for the Greek tradition had made him doubt the Christian God. He may have subscribed to Enlightenment ideals. I can't say, I never asked; I didn't know him well.

In any case those modest suppers—since my aunt certainly never served pheasants and caviar, only white cheese, a little ham, radishes in spring, tomatoes in the summer, jam and good Krakow bread—accompanied the stubborn battles and the jealous looks cast by the lady of the house, baffled by a priest who preferred agnostics to model parishioners.

And the provincial Communist town conquered by Stalin spread out around these arguments, these simple meals. Limousines carried the new regime's dignitaries, men with square faces and unmoving eyes. Countless lectures and discussion groups convened on the nonexistence of God.

The young priest's name was Karol Wojtyla.

People-vowels and people-consonants. Vowels are the ones who like to talk and laugh; they toss back their heads energetically when they laugh, these people born for expression. People-consonants chiefly keep silent, they're known as wet blankets at parties, they fall asleep on trains. But there would be no humanity without them; languages would rather manage without vowels than give up the stiff, heavy brocade of consonants.

A few years ago, perhaps in 1990, I unexpectedly caught sight of Professor U. at the railroad station in Krakow. He was not the potentate he had been. Clad in a shabby gray overcoat, the old man insisted on buying his ticket without standing in line. He launched into a dramatic monologue for the benefit of those people (just a few!) who were waiting ahead of him. He was a poor soul wronged by history, a pensioner who "had once served in an administrative capacity, in other times, to be sure, but some services never die"; he was, in other words, the retiree *tout court*, the prince of pensioners, and simply asked to buy his ticket out of line. I was probably the only one who recognized Professor U. The others, smiling with embarrassment, let the old man through. I was the only one who knew that he was addicted to power and needed to test his strength, to beat others out even in his old age, even at this meager game, by taking two minutes from the lives of others, the two minutes that he himself required—and he'd never hurried in his life— in order to buy a ticket. And a small, sly smile of petty triumph did indeed appear on his face. Professor U. had triumphed once more!

"Friday, December 19, 1945. Prisoners' march from the disbanded camp of Auschwitz through Gliwice. Snow. Very cold.

"Jean Amery was among them. We talked about this in Brussels. I was on the other side. Still a child. I stood at the edge of the sidewalk and stared at those people in stripes. We may have seen each other."—Horst Bienek, *Portrait of a Certain Province.*

I still hadn't been born in January 1945, but by October of that year I'd made my appearance in Gliwice. Years later I got to know Horst Bienek—we talked about Gliwice.

Krakow as seen from another point of view: a small provincial town, consumed by gossip, snobbery, and envy. Each person demands the appropriate title: professor, doctor, engineer, patron of the arts. A small clique of artists, writers, journalists, professors keep close, not always friendly, watch over one another: they know everything there is to know, and then some. The old Communist collectivity has given way to an insatiable drive to unmask your neighbor's slip-ups through a remorseless surveillance not entirely free of envy. Unconcealed curiosity has taken the place of the secret police. A snakes' nest.

All hail the Jagiellonian Library—nicknamed the Jagiellonka—that botanical garden of ideas. Thank you, Jagiello, Jadwiga. It was a treasure trove and only a wall divided it from the busy street. A library—a vast, proud library—embodies the imagination as such, the spirit and intellect of all humanity. Thoughts wait here for future readers. The books pressed close on crowded shelves dream nightly here of contact with readers' living palms. The mundane chain of brief, successive presents doesn't spare even the library: the parquet floors creak each night while the sleepy watchman reads a greasy sports weekly in his tiny office. Before him stands a jar of pickles and some canned sandwich spread; the radio gasps as it spits rippling

music for idiots from its ailing lungs. But the twenty-year-old students come every morning. The library is open daily, except on Sundays and holidays. The students visit the library more often and
more eagerly than the relatives of pensioners turn up at old-age
homes.

The library is an old-age home; the employees are often
unpleasant, even brutal. Thoughtless workers toss the books on
metal carts and tear off at top speed just for fun, as if they were
wearing skates, or carrying the coffin of the town's least favorite
butcher.

The students flock to the library en masse, and their shameless youth fills the books' vessels with its fresh oxygen. Not all
of them, it's true; some are driven in by stern professors. But
that's beside the point. Motivation has never been mankind's
strong suit. Motives may be suspect, fairly low in nature's order,
or even genuinely vile, and still lead to surprisingly lofty results.

Here I studied Plato and Heraclitus, the mysteries of the
Middle Ages, here I read inspired Englishmen, witty Frenchmen,
and morose Germans. As well as my own countrymen. And even
the somber, bearded Russians. And forbidden books, which could
be acquired only with great difficulty, through stratagems and
ruses, or with the dean's permission. That's how I managed to get
ahold of Czeslaw Milosz's poetry and essays.

In Gliwice we lived on Arkonska Street, a modest little street, two
rows of German apartment buildings staring fixedly at each other.
For a long time that little street was the center of my world. From
the balcony I watched the sparks shoot from the coking plants'
smokestacks. Sometimes I caught sight of paratroopers outlined

against the sky as they landed at the nearby air base. Gliders patiently ascended the air's spiral steps.

We lived by turns at number five, seven, and three—ever larger apartments along that same short street. At number seven my neighbor was an awful boy bursting with energy. My mom said nothing good would come of him. His name was Wojtek Pszoniak.

Fall didn't last forever; after a long winter came the spring.

Mr. M. proceeded slowly across the clean parquet gleaming with wax. He had warm slippers on his feet.

It was the era of slipcovers. One had to keep things covered so that they wouldn't wear out. Not just furniture but also clothing, courage, and thoughts. Mr. M. was the perfect embodiment of this thrifty philosophy. He died in the mid-seventies, a retired court clerk, and a modest, thoroughly anonymous person. (I lived at the M.s' place on Urzednicza Street after leaving Mrs. C.) Mr. M. almost never bought new things. On Sundays he'd wear a prewar suit, but otherwise he rarely left the house. He'd happily lie motionless on a sofa in the kitchen, and if he used up anything, it could only be oxygen and time. He had three or four prewar suits, made of first-rate wool, or so he said (and indeed they looked it); and with the assistance of his wife, an unusually deft and industrious individual and a specialist in the habits of moths, he took care that this historic fabric should hold up as long as possible.

On Sunday he and his wife went to church and sometimes took a short walk afterward, weather permitting. He strolled slowly,

cautiously, not like those flighty youngsters who run the risk of
tripping and tearing their jacket or pants. He also thought that you
could walk between the drops in rainstorms. This was his favorite
joke, and not by chance, since it was of a piece with his entire
Weltanschauung.

He perused the local papers lazily, *Echo Krakowa* or *Dziennik
Polski*; he wouldn't so much as touch *Gazeta Krakowska*, which
paraded its Party affiliation on its banner. He was one of those readers whose glasses are usually smeared with a film of grease or a dab
of jam—which didn't bother him at all. Why should he see clearly?
Three sections took all his attention: sports, obituaries, and local
news. He merely skimmed the other columns, without expecting
much by way of news; they could only be improved by the greasy
glasses, which he was always losing anyway, and unhurriedly trying
to find. This search gave him pleasure, since it took a fair amount of
time and helped him while away the day. The day was too long anyway, sixteen hours would have been plenty. The number twenty-
four struck him as arbitrary and arrogant, good enough maybe for
flighty youngsters, but not suitable for retired clerks. He was an
ideal pensioner, passive and resigned.

And he must have been a model clerk in his time. In principle he
had no vices—he didn't drink, didn't stir up trouble. He was exceptionally punctual and industrious. I can only imagine how thoroughly he must have internalized the system of administering
justice, in which he was one of the very smallest pawns. He never
became a judge or prosecutor, or one of those eloquent lawyers he
so admired. But he'd mastered what was perhaps an even harder art;
in his own small life he'd come to embody the virtue of moderation,
of fairness. Judges may pretend to Olympian grandeur, lawyers
may be puffed up, proud, and prosecutors may grow tougher
over time—always asking for the strictest sentence must take a certain psychic toll. Only the modest, irreproachable Mr. M. was

entirely free of these flaws. He classified documents, organized
files seething with perjury and crime, then went home to a well-
earned supper with a measured step and peace in his soul. He
wasn't susceptible to bad examples and rested in the certainty that
the hideous acts he was called upon to classify had nothing to do
with his life. Finally it must be noted that those other, far more visible and renowned agents of justice paid only hasty visits to the
courthouse; they hurriedly donned their robes, and then rushed off
to their chambers as soon as the case was over to meet with their
next client. Whereas the anonymous Mr. M. spent every working
day inside the courthouse and remained outside its walls only on
Sunday.

I hope he never found himself embroiled in those sinister
dilemmas created by a political system that persecuted the innocent, by Communism.

His understanding of history was a bit idiosyncratic. To desig-
nate a change of eras he would say with a slight sneer: "When
democracy set in." It was never quite clear if he meant 1918, when
Hapsburg Austria collapsed, or 1945, when the Communists seized
power. Probably the latter, but I wouldn't stake my life on it. He
was never explicit about his political views; as a pillar of the system
of justice he had to be circumspect, and even in retirement he
maintained his neutrality.

His wife was the person who reconciled him with a defective life
that couldn't be neatly filed away in the judiciary stampbooks. Mrs.
M. never fell beneath feminism's sway and bustled faithfully by her
husband's side. Cooking was her true passion, the real thing, not
simply a labor imposed by an "oppressive spouse." She admitted
openly, "I'm not partial to fruits and vegetables, Mr. Zagajewski, I
favor meat." She made very greasy schnitzels, so greasy that even
my youthful liver rebelled after their consumption. One hates to
think of Mr. M.'s liver! They were both delicious and deadly. Mrs.

M. would have done anything for her husband, she'd have shielded him from any misfortune, but she couldn't deny him—or herself—this one thing: crisp, greasy schnitzels made of ground pork and beef.

Mrs. M. was a kindly, charming soul. She spoke with horror of their flighty neighbor who lived one story up—on the third floor—and who frequently received equally frivolous guests, which placed her, Mrs. M., in an exceptionally compromising position. Because these guests would get mixed up and ring their doorbell, the M.s', without realizing that behind this door lived two people who personified both civic and judicial respectability. Mrs. M. would open the door and quickly realize whom these people—usually tipsy, oozing those prefabricated good spirits induced by alcohol—were really looking for. And she'd show them the way, saying "Up there," and pointing to the third floor. She would laugh about that "Up there," but she was also somewhat embarrassed: Can you believe, I actually showed them the way. And this was her greatest sin, the only one she confessed to me. I doubt there were any others.

Whenever Mr. M. took sick—and his health was quite frail, which drove his adoring wife of many decades to despair—and came down with a fever, he would lie semiconscious on the kitchen daybed and rave about the most overwhelming experience in his life, when he'd fought for the Austrian Army during the First World War, manning a machine gun in the Ukraine. The idea that this peaceful man, the guardian of woolen suits, halfhearted reader of the local papers, and discriminating sports fan, had at one time aimed and fired a machine gun struck me as utterly preposterous, out of the question. I imagined that the prudent Mr. M. must have worked things out even then (but can you really "work things out" in the army?) so that he dealt only with the less aggressive activities, distributing cartridge boxes, for example, or maintaining weapons. Or maybe he confined himself to cooking, supply columns, provisions. But the horror of that time came to life in his stories as though he'd been trapped at the front line. They weren't "stories" in any conventional sense; he spoke of his wartime experiences only when he was feverish. Only a high temperature could force them from his memory's depths until they streamed like lava from a volcano. They weren't stories, since a story gives a certain distance from the past, it adds humor, allows for the possibility of stopping, repeating, retarding the action. But there was no distance here, even though the events had occurred some fifty years earlier. No distance: the Ukrainian steppe, the charging enemy cavalry, the dying horses all appeared in Mrs. M.'s clean white kitchen. His monologues always took place in the summer; and they always featured yellow grain, sheared by machine-gun fire, sun, dust, and death.

But I suspected that Mr. M.—who knew that I "wrote a bit" and had even published poems and reviews—grew delirious partly for my benefit, that perhaps he didn't fend off his wartime memories precisely because he guessed that one day I might write down his ravings, the yellow Ukrainian summer, the horses' shadows vanishing behind the hill, the dust, the machine guns' terrifying whir, orders given in the gentle Austrian German that stifled fear. I don't mean to suggest that his illness was imaginary, that he was playing a part, no, nothing of the sort, but even the humblest hero in a great epic wants to be noticed, to be mentioned in the roster, though he may get only one line, a footnote. The M.s had no children, that was their tragedy; if they had, the Ukrainian battles would have lived on in a younger generation's memory. Mr. M. was no longer young, and I may have been his last chance, his final Homer.

———

The legendary notion of *otium*, known to us only from history books. It's hard for us to imagine what that *otium* was, what state of mind it entailed, what sort of inner freedom it might offer. Release from everyday life and its worries, absorption in reading, peace of mind, intellectual curiosity. Of course, *otium* required wealth, great wealth, a comfortable villa, and a host of baffled servants and slaves to take on the dreary chore of administering the estate. But let's not be too Marxist about it.

That special moment when, after long hours spent in the library's twilight, the half-light of deep thought, you reenter the light of day. For a moment the real world seems unreal. The cheeky green poplars wobble unrealistically. The cars that cross Mickiewicz Boulevard seem to have been cast adrift. The gray sky's reflected in the puddles, and an airplane's tiny dot, not much larger than a swallow's shadow, quivers as it's shaken by a passing foot. For a minute the world seems fraudulent, a cheap deal, a ransom paid to a gang of thieves by a worthy but incompetent creator. The sidewalks are crooked. The earth is round. Man is mortal. Freedom is doubtful.

In some cities the architects who plan libraries have understood the problems inherent in the hazardous passage from a warehouse of living shadows to the reality of a dead life. They have suggested that steps be placed outside the library's entrance, steps on which you can sit out that difficult moment in which you reacclimate to ordinary daylight and pardon the world its homespun imperfection.

Robert Schumann, sonata for violin and piano, first movement, *Mit leidenschaftlichem Ausdruck:* the sonata's form can barely contain its chaotic energy, full of passion and expectation. This is romanticism in its purest form. It's impossible to resist this music even if you prefer classicism's calmer wisdom—which isn't the case for this particular author.

The second movement, the Allegretto, is much shorter and can't bring down the fever of the first part, which assaults the ordered, moderate minds of its auditors. It's astonishing that the first movement can be made to end at all. Its propulsiveness resists all endings and limits.

Mit Energie und Leidenschaft—this is what the first movement is called in Schumann's first piano trio. And just as in the opening movement of the violin sonata, the music's force defies assimilation.

An exhibit of Max Pechstein, the German Expressionist, in a Berlin museum with holdings from the group Die Brücke—a red unknown to nature, the red of rage and expression, the red of rage and rapture. The Expressionists' splendor, the shock I felt at an exhibit of German Expressionists in Paris, 1994, I think: their reds, violets, yellows, their night mixed with the day.

Imagination—that same imagination which brings music and poetry to life—is neither perfect nor self-contained. How often it errs, veers off course, perhaps especially in our day, when it has taken its cue so often from demented ideologies. It needs to work in consort with honesty, common sense, reason—as long as they don't gain the upper hand!

If you try to understand while renouncing expression, you'll understand nothing. If you try to speak without seeking understanding, you'll say nothing.

A certain traveler who knew many continents was asked what he found most remarkable of all. He replied: the ubiquity of sparrows.

I watch old cars, lovely, but also comical. Don't all those thinkers who demonize technology exaggerate just a bit? All you have to do is look at a sixty-year-old car, a thirty-year-old TV set. There's nothing funnier than an old machine.

One way of looking at Paris: I'm sitting in the dentist's waiting room (36, rue de Courcelles) and realize that I've accidentally ended up in the very heart of the Paris built by Baron Haussmann. Through the window I see only Haussmann's Paris, that is, the various sphinxes, lions, and caryatids that adorn enormous apartment houses, including the building on the corner of boulevard Haussmann and rue de Courcelles. It's the least attractive Paris, the monotonous, dark-yellow Paris of the honest bourgeoisie, Napoleon III's ponderous dream, chicken coops for the wealthy. The beautiful Paris surfaces where the city's different strata meet: fragments of medieval structures stand along broad, modern streets, a vast square shaped by Napoleon I abuts a riverside boulevard, where the Seine stretches beneath a vast, clear sky, where rosy chestnuts bloom and people saunter. Certain Parisian streets are masterpieces of civilization. The existentialists may have made boulevard Saint-Germain famous, but its charm owes nothing to existential angst. Just the opposite—this is a street that knows neither fear nor the sickness unto death. It's a street that realizes the miracle of a human race at one with itself, safe and trusting, lost in conversation or in peaceful contemplation, a human race preoccupied by strolling and stopping at bookshop windows. Solitary wanderers gaze at pairs and packs of pedestrians. Clouds show the way and the Seine flows nearby, obediently drifting through the countless combs of stone bridges.

Over the years I've come across a few sentences in Leo Tolstoy's letters that have left their mark on me. In a letter to Alexandra Tolstoy we read: "I'm seized by laughter every time I remember how I used to think—and you apparently still think this—that one might set up a happy, honest little world and lead a peaceful, quiet, faultless life, beyond reproach, serenely doing only what is right. What nonsense! It can't be done, old thing! Any more than one can keep fit without exercise, just by holding still. To live an honest life you must struggle, stray, do battle, make mistakes, begin, give up, start over, quit again, fight and lose without end. Peace is spiritual degradation."

How far we've come from the Stoics' dream, how far this is from Buddhist enlightenment! But it all seems very close to the spiritual landscape we still inhabit today.

Tolstoy's splendid observation doesn't undermine the ideal of wisdom. He simply remarks that this ideal is astronomically difficult to achieve—and to sustain, since life's pace doesn't permit us to keep whatever state we've reached without battle, without sacrifice and defeats.

It must be added, though, that Tolstoy's definition of peace as "spiritual degradation" is a cheap shot, of a piece with his youthful rhetorical bluster. Peace is a port we reach occasionally, sometimes for a long stay, but sooner or later we're always forced to leave, as if our ocean liner sailed beneath a dubious flag pursued by the mistrustful eyes of customs officers.

An old, old friend of mine, Karol Tarnowski, spent several days in Paris. And I heard him play for the first time; he's both a philosopher and a pianist. He gave two concerts, the second of which stayed especially fixed in my mind. It took place in a hall on the fourth or fifth floor of a home for Polish veterans on Legendre Street, number 17. A small audience had gathered in a dusty hall hung with paneling grown dark from sorrow. Counts and countesses, the artist's near and distant relatives, occupied the front rows. Behind them sat a small group of our friends, who'd attended Karol's first performance and decided to come back for more. A long, clear June evening slowly dimmed outside the window. Karol played Bach, Schumann, and Chopin, very beautifully, though the piano was out of tune (Polish veterans clearly don't pay much heed to pianos). But the pianist's struggle with his stubborn instrument didn't ruin the performance, in spite of a few imperfect chords. Just the opposite. It underscored the fine pianist's valor and made the evening that much more memorable. The rapt countesses (as in Chopin's times), including, as it turned out, Madame Potocka; Wojciech (Wojtek) Pszoniak in his long linen coat on the balcony; the unhappy, indisposed piano and the pianist hunched in concentration above its faltering keyboard: what Salle Pleyel recital could compete with such a scene?

———

An orange lay on the table. The shrieks and laughter of children rose from the courtyard below. It was four in the afternoon.

One of language's most uncanny features is its capacity to suggest— if only through allusion, through approximation—the way the world's been built on an abyss. It is neither safe nor solid; it lacks a ground floor, a foundation. What would happen if architects, for example, took on the task of expressing the world's vertiginous instability? They'd need to erect crooked buildings . . . No, more than this, they'd be forced in principle to put up structures that collapsed at a precisely scheduled hour, to burrow tunnels deep into the earth that served no purpose but to demonstrate to the general public the approximate nature of the void. What if the people in charge of arranging timetables for trains decided to expose the metaphysical cracks in our existence? They'd have to schedule regular train crashes, and bridges would need to be blown up periodically. Painters would be obliged to perforate their canvases, while cobblers would append tiny, predictable bombs to our footwear. In every other sphere of activity such experiments would constitute inhuman sabotage. Doctors would damage their patients (not all that uncommon, alas). Even music's strict, cast-iron structures couldn't withstand an alarm clock's ringing out to signal the abyss. Only language can play host to such sabotage without itself becoming party to the destruction. Just the opposite—it helps us to tame a force that otherwise refuses to be tamed.

There are two sciences, one under the sign of fire and the other beneath the sign of air. The first deals with revelation, divinity; its teachers are volumes of poetry with yellowed pages, empty country churches, certain works of music, and moments of loneliness during long walks. It's an impractical science; we don't know what to do with its prescriptions, how to integrate them into life. And how can we integrate this science into life when it itself is life? When next to its fervor all else fades into ashes, tedium, routine? This science is consumed by passion and at times by envy; it apparently can't abide the other sciences, or simply ignores them.

The second science—beneath the sign of air—is intensely level-headed. It is taken up chiefly with thoughts on the distribution of wealth. This distribution, which should ideally be equitable, is the primary, praiseworthy preoccupation of this science (an indispensable science for any society). Unfortunately, this sober science knows nothing—or next to nothing—about the nature of the treasures it's intent on handing out. This is the task of the first science (the one beneath the sign of fire), which is so absorbed in these treasures that it can't bear to think of sharing them, not from stinginess, but from passion. The second science wants to share, but has no idea what it's sharing! Funny, isn't it?

Karol Tarnowski's visit and our conversations reminded me of a meeting we had many years ago, when I was still a student, a meeting that turned out to be immensely important to me. I first got to know him through his wife, Marysia, who happened to be my cousin. Karol belonged then—through his family and friends—to the Catholic circle centered on *Tygodnik powszechny* and *Znak*, two superb journals grudgingly tolerated by the Communists. Both *Tygodnik powszechny* and *Znak* stood for an intelligent, liberal, non-nationalistic Catholicism, a faith that was nonetheless fervent, undiluted by rationalistic concessions. These were exceptional people, Europeans, cultivated, brave. Jerzy Turowicz, an absolutely honest man, was *Tygodnik's* editor in chief for many years. That such a group of people could exist and even put out books and periodicals within the Soviet empire verged on the miraculous. The authorities harassed them, restricted their papers' circulation, and limited the editions of those few books that managed to make it past the censors—but they allowed them to exist. One office actually existed for *Tygodnik powszechny*, another actually existed for *Znak*, and these two truly extant rooms, which you could actually enter, where you could remove your real jacket, take a real seat, drink actual tea, and hold a conversation with free people—these two rooms made life easier. It wasn't a religious phase of my life. Only ashes, traces remained from childhood's ecstasies. But I don't think I'd fallen prey to the state's ubiquitous, insidious campaign against the Church. I'd yielded to myself instead, to youth's inalienable right to a spiritual crisis in the sixteenth year of life, when a new person begins to emerge from the old (the only truly "new person" whom we'll ever really see; the twentieth century's doctrines may have promised the birth of a "new person," but he still hasn't made his debut, and just as well). If any external influence had reached me, it wasn't official propaganda but rather the dark literature of our century, the century now drawing to a close. I'd devoured Kafka and Beckett; I'd even given a brief report on the theater of the absurd in high school. I scoured the journals *Tworczosc* and *Dialog*, and tracked the progress of art's black vision. The state monitored and harassed the Church; but the Church was triumphantly present nonetheless in nearly every family's private life. Its success in Communist Poland was the more striking since the Catholicism that packed the churches every Sunday must have seemed a mere bourgeois ideal, a paragon for *bien pensants*, to many students like myself, driven by the eternal, often erring, instincts of young artists to seek out nonconformity at any cost (thus running the risk of becoming the most commonplace conformists). I rediscovered my earlier responsiveness to religion only much later, as an adult.

I wasn't one of those students who attended the semilegal meetings of the university's clergy. I got to know the people connected with *Tygodnik powszechny* only after finishing my studies, through Karol Tarnowski. Karol's half brother, Jacek Wozniakowski, was one of the first I met: a charming man, wonderfully intelligent and learned. Some years later *Znak* helped me through a rough time—I was a dissident, and unemployed—and I came to know almost all the inhabitants of the island that was *Tygodnik powszechny*. Party representatives dismissively called them the "church vestibule." The term held hidden envy as well as contempt, since they must have suspected that these people, unlike themselves, were free; if anyone was cooped up in a vestibule, it was these party lackeys, who fed on pathetic gossip involving microscopic twitches and shifts in the vast massif of power ("Lukasiewicz hasn't turned up in public for a month; Szlachcic's gone off to Moscow," "What do you think it means," et cetera).

Religious ardor wasn't my strong suit back then, but I was impressed by the quality of these people. (Some of them had just one shortcoming; they overrated the right they'd received to travel quite freely throughout Europe and the world. As a result they began shunning dissidents toward the end of the seventies; they feared being infected with the dissidents' loss of privileges.) I admired their calm courage, their humor, their singularity.

In the mid-seventies, when the organized opposition first arose, a program in civic education was established and arranged by grades and years. It drew, naturally enough, upon the resources of the second science, the science of distribution.

But you shouldn't praise language too highly, since even language can be completed only by what lies outside it. Like us, language draws upon what lies beyond it. It's like a homeless soul seeking sustenance. And it is this sustenance that brings life, not language alone.

Mr. K., an elegantly dressed older man with a cowlick springing stubbornly from his lofty brow, was our lecturer in economics; he mocked capitalist theories once weekly. Capitalism is doomed to extinction, please make a note, ex-tinc-tion. The accumulation of capital leads unfailingly to disaster. He enjoyed digressions: just imagine, he'd say, Professor Ingarden was slaving away on his *Debate Over the Existence of the World* just as we were building Nowa Huta. Don't you see? Ingarden wasn't sure if the world really existed at the very moment that we were busily digging foundations, building apartment houses, shovels glistening, pickaxes striking rocks, and the world existed, glittering in the morning sun like a diamond.

Is Mr. K. even worth mentioning? His shape scarcely differs from the thousands of other bustling little figures happily fulfilling Party orders. He did have one distinctive feature: he had a little imagination, he liked avant-garde painting and even occasionally bought the artworks of the Krakow Group. And he showed up regularly at the painters' openings. He was a perfect example of a functionary who'd been domesticated, demoralized by Krakow, tainted by the city's snobbery.

Capitalism took up three quarters of the monumental text-book of political economy that was Mr. K.'s bible and his students' bane. Socialism, on the other hand, was discussed in the imperative mood and the future tense: the planned economy will flourish . . . overtake . . . The production of consumer goods will be raised to the level . . . But the textbook never mentioned what was actually going on, since the real economy of the time consisted in getting by, not going out, sparing your old clothes. Living as little as possible. The elbows of sweaters and jackets were shielded with prophylactic patches. One of my uncles used to proclaim the following philosophical maxim in all seriousness: We're too poor to buy cheap things. But we were too poor to buy anything.

Even the seasons seemed to lend themselves to this stingy economy. A hurried, hectic period stretched from April until July, that creative season cynically described by scholars as the reproductive cycle. Birds sang, leaves peeped coquettishly from sticky buds, tomcats howled in the courtyards. And then it suddenly grew still, the second half of July proceeded under the sign of silence. Blackbirds busily repaired their nests; spring's rampant romanticism made way for classical autumn. Green fields yielded to yellow stubble. The issue wasn't surplus but survival.

The world's inexhaustible duality, that is, poetry and prose. "Everything is poetry," Edward Stachura liked to say; but he was wrong. Poetry always lives next door to prose, just as the sacred exists only when juxtaposed to the profane. The day starts with a moment of poetry, as the first ray of sun begins to shine, but then come long hours of arduous morning. Alarm clocks ring, sleepy mothers make coffee for their unconscious offspring. Helena takes the first streetcar out to the center for rat control. Paris commuter trains bulge with millions of white-collar workers rushing off to offices. Dark clouds drift over Krakow and Paris (it's still pitch-black in Houston). Only around ten o'clock, after all the factory and office workers have had their first coffee or tea, does poetry cautiously creep back, checking to see that the coast is clear.

Poetry will never conquer prose's dominion. But this doesn't necessarily mean that prose will vanquish the terrain of poetry.

But there are many—too many!—states of mind that don't lend themselves to poetry, that demand ironic, even mocking prose. This is why I sometimes understand Cioran's comment: "I go through periods when I'm deaf to mysticism and poetry. Lyricism, in whatever form, has the effect of an emetic on me. Only spiteful, foul-tempered prose can give me pleasure."

You need two things to build a nation, strength and weakness. To write a good book also takes strength and weakness.

Amid the sea of loquacity produced by the Genevan diarist Amiel you occasionally come upon a lovely sentence like this one: *Une parole dite à quelqu'un conserve un effet indestructible, comme un mouvement quelconque se métamorphose sans s'anéantir.* (A word spoken to someone is indestructible, like energy, which doesn't die but only changes shape.)

But there are words and words—some vanish in five minutes, while others live forever. No linguistic theory can explain the difference between them, between "words, words, words"—it's worth noting that this ironic line turns up in one of world literature's most enduring works—and the word that lives on, both static and in constant motion, proof against time, ridicule, and irony (though not against neglect!). Clearly, linguistic theories treat not the word but language.

Once, in Paris, we were chatting with an elderly couple, the owners of an inexpensive jewelry store. It turned out they were Polish and had lived in Gliwice after the war. But they had found happiness only in Paris, since, they told us, speaking in chorus as happy, too happy, married pairs are wont to do, for all those years in Poland we made only enough to keep body and soul together. And not a penny more. But we multiplied our capital, and not just once, for the first time here in Paris.

I nodded my head dutifully on hearing their two-headed tale, but I actually wanted to laugh. They'd wanted to increase their capital in a Communist country, impoverished and worn down by ideology! What lack of subtlety! I found myself thinking afterward, though, that they were just normal people, after all, not intellectuals poring over Blake or Marx at night, just solid chthonic citizens from the country of the moon (as opposed to the country of the sun). Increasing capital in Gliwice! In Communist Poland! In a land as flat as an empty glove!

The reality of wool and that of the finished suit; that's how one might see the relationship of history as we know it in deeds, in action, in textbooks, and history as unused potential. We're not likely to outrun history, even if we try, even if we do come across those moments, common enough, that music especially but also poetry and painting sometimes provide, the moments that seem to free us from history's orbit, that set us circling through a calmer, more congenial space. Such moments are completely valid, but we can't stay there forever. We can't escape from historicity the way the Jews fled Egypt. We can't get rid of it for good. More than this—historicity has its attractions. Let's pass over this century's terrors for a moment; through its historicity art gives access to transformations, discoveries, innovations, quests, investigations, and, afterward, homecomings, return trips to what had come before, to tradition. You have only to imagine a music that never went beyond Gregorian chants. Let's imagine that Gregorian chants, which were themselves preceded by centuries of music and dance, are the music of timelessness, of ahistorical, static, blissful, sweet eternity.

I love listening to Gregorian chants, but I can't endure the thought of losing all stylistic evolution, development, change, of losing Bach and Monteverdi, Mozart and Beethoven, Chopin, Mahler, Stravinsky, Lutoslawski, and so many splendid composers. It's past bearing. Just Gregorian chants, thousands of hours of chanting, patient, peaceful, repetitive chanting! No—we're better off with historicity and its endless progression, its restless changes, its revolutions and restorations.

On the other hand, though, we shouldn't be slaves to historicity. We shouldn't think that things could never turn out otherwise in the history of politics, art, music, literature. We must keep in mind the vast supplies of wool from which our suits are made. Rough bales of that wool, secured against time's ravages, are packed in scrupulously guarded warehouses. My guess is that their stockrooms don't just contain the wool for coming centuries. They also store the unused wool of distant times, the wool of events that never came to pass, nations that were never realized, cities that remained unbuilt, the wool of people who were never born, of those who died too soon, of those whose lives didn't turn out, the wool of unwritten epics and symphonies, of unpainted pictures, of thoughts that never came to mind, the wool of a world in which fate worked differently. The wool of a slightly different humanity, less envious, less petty. This wool gives us strength. We don't see it, we can't touch it, but it gleams, it gives us energy and joy. We don't know how it happens, how it's possible for secret rays and signs to pass through the beams of these sturdy warehouses, but that's how it is. Wool of the Argonauts. The golden fleece.

The world's duality? Partitions into poetry and prose? Isn't this just a little too easy? Wouldn't we be better off trying to unify reality in such a way that nobody could beg off, saying, "So sorry I couldn't help, but that day I happened to be in prose's jurisdiction, not in the domain of poetry"? Shouldn't we seek out at all costs the force that joins together, not the one that drives apart? Shouldn't we raise up what is low and not simply resign ourselves, retreat, continue to justify all the defects of this dichotomous division? Aren't day and night enough? Why cut when you can paste?

There is a certain kind of stern wisdom that takes the shape of assessing another's actions, of praise or condemnation ("He betrayed . . . a worthless man . . . so generous . . ."). This judgment is more than mere moral evaluation; it conveys something irreversible, something completely authentic. Such wisdom has no home in philosophy. Neither Kant, nor Descartes, nor Husserl was able to build such a home. A judgment of this sort may be voiced by an old woman in a train (someone whom we'll never see again), by a very young person, or even—it's been known to happen—by a philosopher. Truth is homeless.

But you should also bear in mind that such judgments may make a tremendous impression upon us at first, and then prove to be utterly unjust, mistaken, partisan, ad hoc. Truth is doubly homeless.

Simone Weil's most compelling feature—I'll have to put this rather awkwardly—is the sense she conveys that she alone in all the twentieth century has actually managed to build just such a philosophical abode for stern human truth. But she herself errs so often . . . Truth is always homeless.

Apart from Weil, there is Dietrich Bonhoeffer, one of the very few who spoke as though they possessed the gift of making a home for truth. And one of those who perished before he'd finished building.

The barbarism of my countrymen: my countrymen, who cry out if the Lyczakowski Cemetery in Lwow suffers the slightest damage, leveled almost every German cemetery in the western territories that were added after the war; they tore down German tombstones, erased German inscriptions, dishonored German graves, buried their own dead in someone else's soil, and killed the memory of those who had long dwelled in these burial grounds.

———

Gombrowicz never gets to the heart of the matter in his attack on poetry (*Against Poets*). He'd have been right if he'd just kept to the occupational hazards of poetry: an eternal poetic inebriation, amplified at times by the incapacity for sober, critical thought that so often afflicts poets, who are prone to emulating children. Or else they get poetry mixed up with sports.

But a defense of poetry isn't meant to defend a single profession, bookshops, bibliophiles, impressionable readers, readings for an audience of twenty. It's not even a defense of poets, who are about as distant from poetry as lawyers are from the law or mountain climbers from the clouds. To defend poetry means to defend a fundamental gift of human nature, that is, our capacity to experience the world's wonder, to uncover divinity in the cosmos and in another human being, in a lizard, in chestnut leaves, to experience astonishment and to stop still in that astonishment for an extended moment or two. The human race won't perish if this capacity withers—but it will be weaker, worse off, different from what it was throughout those millennia when every civilization placed poetry, in whatever form, at the heart of all human endeavor.

I don't know if I'm the only one who's struck by fear, by uncertainty, each December as the old year draws to a close and the year's last night awaits us, the night whose stillness, the pristine stillness of a winter's evening, we seek to stifle with firecrackers, loud music, and erupting bottles of champagne. Anxiety seizes me, I worry that suddenly everything will change, and I'll change too in some unforeseeable way, and so will everyone dear to me, and even the world itself won't stay the same. But then January begins, the damp snow falls, and it turns out that nothing has changed, at least for now. It's a miracle, the miracle of identity, one of our very few weapons against time. It's a deceptive weapon; we all know that time will win in the end (or will it?), time, as impartial as a Chinese philosopher, an infinitely patient chess player, a Croesus stockpiling millions and billions of years in his capacious deep freezers.

And yet—you meet someone you haven't seen for ten years and he's exactly the same as he was. True enough, he stoops a bit, he's grown grayer and thinner, but he's still *exactly the same*. In Nabokov's novels, take *Pnin*, for example, the same scene comes up time and again: the hero meets his beloved many years hence. The scene is an experiment conducted in life's laboratory, a duel between omnivorous time and the principle of identity. In Nabokov the moment of recognition confirms a triumphant conviction: *she* is *exactly the same*, time hasn't managed to change a thing.

Twenty-year-old students talking poetry and philosophy until dawn, sitting in a cheap café in a garret in Krakow or Paris: who can match their ardor, who can defend or indict all writers, living and dead, with greater passion? No one better honors the works of the human spirit than students sitting for hours in the smoke-filled rooms of little restaurants, students caught up in conversation.

One day I heard the bells. They rang every day, but I couldn't always hear them. They rang for vespers. They rang out so loudly that they stifled every thought and whim; the bodies of pedestrians became mobile sound boxes. Krakow possessed vast funds of bells, bells in countless numbers, with the lord mayor of bells, the Zygmunt Bell, at their helm. The Zygmunt Bell sounded rarely, it waited for major, exceptional occasions; ordinarily, though, it dozed in the cathedral tower like a pensioner. Whereas other, lesser bells swung gleefully, like gymnasts on parallel bars. The air quivered frantically, and our bodies quivered with it. The Middle Ages suddenly returned, a late medieval afternoon, and the totalitarianism of bells, fear and joy, every molecule and cell, was vibrating: get to church, time for church, or so some historians would read this sound. But ringing bells aren't pragmatic, and shouldn't be reduced to commands or requests alone. This ringing merely makes the air's latent, inner trembling both immanent and audible. It divulges the air's hidden nature. Some passersby clapped their palms to their ears, shielding them; they couldn't bear the ringing. Others grumbled that the bells woke them at dawn, or didn't let them watch TV, or kept them from getting to sleep. Once I heard someone complain on French radio about the shamelessness of bells. But I didn't cover my ears; the deluge of bells made me happy. The bells gave me a moment of happiness; thanks to them I understood once more that greatness exists in spite of my laziness, in spite of those long spells when I forgot all about it; it slipped my mind for weeks on end as I got lost in other projects, grew preoccupied by other cares and longings. The bells woke me to a higher life.

From conversations with the dead: "You don't know, you can't imagine what vast, celestial pleasure eating an ordinary apple brings. Yes, an ordinary apple. No, there are no ordinary apples."

The fatal flaw that marked most of our teachers wasn't their adherence to the Party line; they were civilized, "European" Marxists, not crude Stalinists (hence their comic snobbery as they stressed the Western European, not Soviet, pedigree of their ideas—it was always Gramsci, Lucien Goldmann, Althusser, Tawney). No—they were anti-Midases, and diminished everything they touched.

She looked toward the window attentively, as if expecting an answer or sign. She grasped the window frame with the fingers of her right hand, just to be sure. The daylight was both blurry and intense. She couldn't make out any details. More than this—it was absolutely quiet, as if the city's streets were padded with a thick layer of snow.

Finally she understood: I'm only a figure in a painting by Vermeer.

After a while I realized that I'd been born in a century which, for some unknown reason, had been generous to its ironists but had dealt less kindly with the moralists, endowing them, for the most part, with middling abilities at best and virtually no sense of form.

From time to time I'd enter one of Krakow's churches and catch some of the sermon; the poor priests were generally talentless, lacking both the gift of oratory and any notion of form. Both the priests and the speakers from various charitable institutions gave talks full of good intentions but devoid of inspiration, talks inadvertently tainted with cant and artificial rapture. They weren't hypocrites—even if it sometimes seemed that way—but they lacked that particular gift of language which saves us from mendacity, or rather, from the appearance of mendacity. They lacked form. Only skeptics and mockers have by and large been endowed with a sense of form, as if the world had abruptly contracted (at odds with the theory of cosmic expansion!) and could see itself only in morose, laconic miniature. The good-hearted speakers relied on truisms; their appeals were amorphous, inflated. Krakow's priests were professional moralists with no interest in language; they hadn't spent enough time on metaphor, metonymy, and syntax; they had no feel for our ironic age's artistic tendencies. They inevitably lost out to those sarcastic artists who had grasped the era's spirit.

Poor priests, poor moralists—they lifted their eyes skyward and recited their sermons as they'd learned to in their seminaries, in a droning, priestly voice, with no sense of humor, no sense of defeat.

Each of us is born, though, with a star, whose light is strong and constant—we have only to keep faith with that star. But you also need talent, which isn't in the stars; it's in the sun, the air, the water, in birdsong, the murmur of tall grasses.

One lecturer specialized in Pavlov. Dogs and reflexes, both conditioned and unconditioned, were his field, and he knew it inside and out. He knew everything about Pavlovism. Another was a logician, who drew signs on the blackboard corresponding to various series which devoured each other in turn like fishes. We also learned that there is a greater and a smaller quantifier: this was interesting. Still another professor lectured on statistics and demonstrated once a week how to count and calculate everything that can't be counted. He was fond of the Gaussian curve, which forms, as we all know, a bell; perhaps it evoked a faint echo of bygone religious sentiments.

I had both high and low before me. As in any city. The two elements were neighbors, friendly or hostile. Art galleries and Renaissance churches promenaded through the old town, but right next door, by the railroad station, stout, aging prostitutes reigned beside their rowdy, drunken suitors. Communism claimed, as I recall, to have stamped out the plague of prostitution, but those florid caryatids had never read the papers and didn't know they were extinct.

In the first days of November, when the dead had just received their modest gifts (always the same chrysanthemums), swing made its way from Warsaw to Krakow. Bearded jazz musicians turned up in our quiet town, wearing thick sheepskins and carrying cases in which gleaming metal instruments took their rest. Surgical equipment could no doubt be constructed of such metal.

The same crowd always showed up at their concerts, equally bearded auditors in equally thick sheepskins, which shielded them both from the cold and from the commonplace, from ordinary life. Nothing was worse than ordinary life. Daily life, days trotting lazily along, the life embraced by the parents and siblings of the bearded trumpeters and drummers, and of their faithful listeners, must have struck them as monstrous, inhuman. Jazz seemed to offer refuge from this calamity. To get up in the morning, go to work, come home from work, eat dinner at the same time daily, dream generally acknowledged dreams—this was synonymous with defeat. (And this is genuinely unpleasant, but, as one philosopher said, "It's better than nothing.")

Jazz was something else again. Jazz is the music of metal. The trumpet of Clifford Brown or Chet Baker, the saxophone of Charlie Parker or Paul Desmond. Metal isn't sentimental. (Of course, there are those intensely sentimental saxophonists who gratify the hormonal emotions of sixteen-year-old sweethearts, but that's not what I'm talking about.) The instruments resting in the musicians' cases were built of metal: surgical implements that held the rhythmic, twisted melody of jazz. There's something cold in Dizzy Gillespie's dialogues with Charlie Parker; metals talking among themselves, metals that first meet above the earth; they had anticipated their conversation years earlier, while they were still dispersed in veins of ore, while they lay compacted in scattered deposits, flattened beneath the press of mountain massifs (people and metals travel in opposite directions—metals emerge from the earth whereas we gradually head underground). You catch a similar voice at times when trumpets play in Bach. And it's because metals are mute and indifferent by nature, removed from art—the strings of a violin or cello are distinctly organic in origin—that we find their voice so stirring.

Jazz can't be compared with the ocean of classical music, with its vast repertoire of tones. Jazz has only one way of producing sound. There are moments, though, when jazz alone becomes a metaphor for freedom. Jazz phrases serve as summonses to greater boldness, to risk. "Don't worry! Who cares about the neighbors!" says the jazz trumpet, says the trumpet's metal. And there's something commanding in its voice.

Jazz phrases fly from the rhythm section's texture like birds from thick-leaved plane trees. Sometimes they're brief, like the scraps of conversation that wake us in small-town hotels. Metals rush to tell their lives, especially in their dialogues with other instruments.

Brass instruments never receive this kind of freedom in orchestras. Even Mahler, who understood metal's sensibilities so well, who reckoned with the agelong domination of the strings, organic and plaintive, failed to liberate completely the orchestra's right hemisphere. You had to listen to jazz in order to hear metal speaking, in order to experience the piercing voice of chrome-plated steel, the hiss of brass, the mood swings of nickel.

Metals slide across the inner life without expressing it, as the cello, for example, might. Sometimes I feel the need for metallic

sounds; in jazz you can hear knives singing. Knives rip the psy-
che's fabric to shreds and strengthen it in the process. (Forgive
me, cellos!)

The bearded jazz musicians came. A few Swedes. Englishmen.
At times a real American. And our own musicians, who took nicknames like Joe or Stanley, since their polysyllabic Slavic names
(Bogumil . . . Wladyslaw . . . Stanislaw) didn't suit jazz's hard matter. These All Souls' Days would start up late at night, usually in
Gothic cellars, which the city had in abundance. They were meant
to start very late—this was the plan—and then on top of that they'd
be delayed; the demigods always kept you waiting. Then finally
they'd appear, wrapped in thick furs or sheepskins, since November
was usually cold, and even when it wasn't, fur coats were chic. Furs
and sheepskins, like extra cases. Beaver. Shaggy furs, soft sheepskins, warm sweaters, as if to underscore the distance between this
warm shell and the metal voice of jazz. Then they finally started
playing and, as the bass dryly kept time and the drums marked the
minutes of a new life, the alto saxophone announced that the metals
would sing yet another whetted song, would slice and cut our warm
thoughts once again.

Where can the inner life be, a certain student of philosophy won-
dered, when the world is so jam-packed with outer life? I set out on a
long walk; first I go past the department stores. Hustle and bustle
everywhere—even people who aren't buying fall prey to the -
prevailing agitation. Even people with no wares to hawk look as if
they might start yelling any minute. Then I head toward the river.
No peace there either. Barges swim up and down the river. Little
shipyards stretch along both banks, building boats and steamers. I
change directions and set out for the hills. I reach the outskirts,

reach the spot where the city turns, almost imperceptibly, into the countryside. Sturdy brick villas give way to smaller houses, encircled by large, well-nourished barns.

Tractors, chatty as newspaper vendors, trundle across the highway. Wagons full of hay trudge toward the farms. There's no inner life here, there isn't room for it. And farther on, where fields and copses stretch, where the forest's dark realm starts, I don't find any empty space; you'll just come across crows, hares, foxes, weasels, and roe deer there. I return to the city; I look at the enormous buildings full of offices and banks. Computer screens flicker in the windows. It's not here. Once home, I open a book of poems and think with relief that here at least I won't be disappointed. But there's no inner life even here, only metaphors and similes, some beautiful and moving, others lackluster or trite. I go to a museum. I look at canvases depicting landscapes, still lifes, or human faces, or sometimes merely colored spots. I like some of them very much, but I still don't find what I'm after.

Even within me, the student of philosophy mused, echoes and reflections of the world predominate. I'm like the pictures in the city museum: filled with the faces and voices of others. What if the inner life doesn't really exist?

The lights in the censorship bureau shone late into the night. The censors couldn't go home with the rest, they had to wait for late editions of the papers, for the evening theater. Later, when I had earned the somewhat doubtful privilege of eating in the journalists' cafeteria, I used the opportunity to scrutinize the censors, who also ate there. Some journalists wouldn't eat at the same table as the censors. But the censors saw their calling as no less honorable than journalism; they considered themselves journalists of a higher order, metajournalists, stylists really, who corrected the errors of ordinary laborers using ordinary pens. But they drank heavily after dinner, the way people drink when they're trying to forget. A few dutiful journalists would join them. And they'd forget.

The philosophy student was right up to a point: the inner life can't be seen or touched. You may bravely give your life up to the hunt; it still eludes all pursuers. But this isn't because it doesn't exist; it's because it always feeds on something new. In a certain sense, the very phrase "the inner life" is imprecise. It is in fact within us, but it's in ceaseless conversation with what lies outside. It's always directed toward the outer world, and exists only in dialogue with a small or great transcendence.

In the same way, meditation doesn't think about itself, and contemplation doesn't contemplate itself.

I was twenty-three; someone advised me to apply to the Society of Atheists and Freethinkers and offer my services as a lecturer. Their honoraria were very high. A short, demonic man received me. A demon of cynicism, not of intellect. Oh yes, he said, we pay very well. But we're paying for the promulgation of rationalist attitudes, the consolidation of secular humanism, the eradication of fideism. But I kept my presence of mind—or perhaps it was my conscience—and said that issues of atheism weren't in my line, and I wasn't qualified to give lectures on "The Death of God," "Why There Is No God," "Why Religion Is Not Simply Superfluous But Harmful," "Catholicism in the Face of a Rapidly Changing Society," or "The Atheist's Ethos" (the lecture sub-

jects were given in a letter, and each "lecturer" could pick appropriate topics), and would rather talk on "Ethics and Morality" or
"The Situation of Poetry in the Contemporary Social Landscape."
The man looked at me scornfully; no doubt he preferred militant activists, kamikaze ideologues to the timid advocates of half
measures.

I remember two trips; the first took me, I think, to Kety, a small
town near Krakow. I remember the smell of the chilly bus I took to
Kety. I was supposed to give a lecture in some sort of factory, I don't
remember what kind. My audience had gray, tired faces. I don't
know if they got an hour off work or if they had to attend a lecture
by their "Krakow comrade" after their shift was over. "Comrade,"
of course, since the local sponsors didn't suspect that their guest
had chosen the mildest of topics, that he'd never belonged to the
Party and had no intention of joining, that he belonged to a different tribe entirely, and was just a young poet trying to make enough
money to buy some books and records. And so I spoke to these tired
people (their faces were truly ashen), whose ranks included more
women than men, explaining the difference between descriptive
sentences and moral propositions, the structure of moral propositions, the disputes on the existence of ethical values, and G. E.
Moore's intriguing observations.

I repeated the received wisdom I'd picked up at the university—
for an hour, perhaps fifty minutes—while my audience either dozed
or stared stubbornly out of the window. It was an autumn day, over-
cast and ugly, as gray as the workers' complexions. When I'd finished, I asked for questions. But there were no questions. Someone,
probably the regional Party secretary, thanked me for my "stimu-
lating lecture," and I went back the same day to Krakow, wondering
what to spend my money on, a history of philosophy or Brahms's
Third Symphony, or maybe on a new edition of Shakespeare's
plays. And whether I should be ashamed of it.

Roman Ingarden was the philosophers' god. He'd already retired by the time I started my studies, but he stopped by the department regularly, like an aging nobleman who no longer governs his estate but still takes an interest in the fruits produced by the legacy that he's passed on to a younger generation. He was able to function normally at the university, to conduct classes without making concessions to the prevailing doctrine of base and superstructure: this was one of Krakow's great surprises. He was rather short and had the handsome head of an elderly gentleman. This student of Husserl, the author of subtle studies on the nature of artworks, was also renowned for his marvelous lectures. His former students tried to describe Ingarden's manner to those unfortunates who'd come too late to experience his charisma, precision, and eloquence firsthand.

"One time he had a pitcher of water in front of him. He started talking about it, an insignificant pitcher, not even crystal, with such force that after an hour or so this humble pitcher—you wouldn't have given it a second glance ordinarily, in a junk shop you'd have ignored it completely, gone looking for prettier pitchers or secondhand beads—had become more beautiful for us than all the palaces of the Emperor of India (even if there is no such person). All he had to do was trace the shape of a chair with his hand, like a painter, and the chair stood there before us. When he was in good form, well rested, not under fire from the administration, it seemed as though he were creating objects with the wave of his hand, bringing them into being."

"He was a great poet, a poet of objects. Sometimes he'd talk about the role of everyday things in our lives, how we treat them, how they dwell with us, seemingly tamer than the friendliest dog or cat. But we never see them whole, they always hold a certain mystery, a side we can't see, and for them this is perhaps their key, their root, their heart, their core. We'd relinquish our mundane sense of

reality; and the barrier that divided the dull, everyday trappings of
the lecture hall from the worlds created by Professor Ingarden
would disappear. Once, after he'd given one of his most inspired
lectures on the life of objects (and when he talked about objects he
was really talking about our world), he took a fountain pen from his
jacket's inner pocket, probably to jot down a few words, one of the
little discoveries he'd made for us in the course of that unforgettable, endlessly generous hour. But we couldn't suppress a muffled
sigh of rapture: that beautiful fountain pen, black and shining, suddenly struck us as an object from legend, from another species of
beings, from a family in which its brother was the unicorn and its
sister was the nymph Calypso."

"The phenomenological epoche (you know, Husserl's famous
suspension of judgments and convictions) became in his articula-
tion, his performance—I've picked this word because there was
something in his lectures that called to mind a first-class actor,
subtle and almost imperceptible—something close to an artist's
inspiration. As if abandoning our everyday convictions could lead
to a strange state of bliss, almost a trance."

"He was a magician. As soon as he'd start talking about an
orange, its roundness, and how we'd never see its other side (as you
probably know, the classic revelation of phenomenology), it would
appear before us. We'd see it quite clearly, a tempting, fragrant
orange globe, full of juice and eternal youth, an orange in a state of
perfect turgor."

All the more so, I'd add quietly to myself, so as not to dampen
my colleagues' ardor (they were older than I was, but still very
young students), all the more so since it was a time when oranges
weren't to be found in those grim government produce shops that
called to mind musty, forsaken herbaria, full of dead, dry stalks and
brown leaves, more than tropical gardens. Ingarden's listeners must
have been primed, like the participants in a séance, to oblige their

instructor by completing the materialization of the suggested object.

My skepticism was no doubt tinged by a powerful streak of envy; I'd missed my chance forever to hear the great master lecture! It wasn't fair—the poetry of objects drew me too, it summoned me. I knew of it chiefly through the verses of Zbigniew Herbert, but my own private meetings with objects had also pointed me toward it. I interrogated every student who remembered the hours spent with Ingarden, I wanted to find out every detail, every miracle that had taken place in that small, cozy hall still heated by an enormous tile stove with a mind of its own, and not by some fine-ribbed central heating system manned by unseen hands.

Unfortunately, the tales of Ingarden's former students were no match for the lectures of the master—how could they be?—and so I'll never know precisely what gave his teaching its magic. Their conscientious accounts lacked one key element: the genius of the old philosopher, who was not just a scholar but a sorcerer. Moreover, after a while the senior students grew tired of trying to answer my endless pleas for new details. Their stories disappointed me; they were stronger on awe than they were on specificity, but that awe was fed by memories to which I had no direct access. What use to me was rapture that couldn't provide proof or proffer documents, that didn't take the shape of coherent narratives, that didn't inspire my friends, that wasn't contagious? They rummaged through their young memories like collectors browsing through albums of rare stamps. Their intentions were good—but they couldn't just invite me, after all, to walk the long pathways of their minds in quest of those niches where they'd stored the mute statuettes of recollections some two or three years old.

So I had to rely on myself, on my own imagination. And things reached the point where I was ready to swear, like a small child, that Ingarden had actually, literally brought objects into being before the very eyes of his admiring auditors, and afterward some limping janitor had grumbled under his breath about all the trouble that crazy philosopher gave him, as if they'd pay him overtime for hauling scores of pale, dead objects out of the classroom after every lecture (not even my imagination could enable Ingarden to create things that lasted like the products of those famous Japanese factories, with their sturdy, long-term guarantees). But these lifeless objects each possessed, nonetheless, that moment of glory when they had briefly emerged from oblivion to glow, for an instant, like crown jewels.

I knew, of course, that phenomenology hadn't set out to create glittering new objects but to shine a new light on the things that already existed. (Husserl's endless, bloated tracts awakened a powerful hunger for objects among poets and writers, as if he'd realized that people were beset by a sea of language, a surfeit of ideas. But of course he himself played a shell game with things, concealing them beneath a thick blanket of sophistic German theory.) And the extraordinarily resourceful Ingarden distinguished himself precisely in this domain, or so his students, witnesses to the master's exploits, assured me. He restored things, made them strange and new once more. But, once again, his auditors, at least those with whom I spoke, my fellow students, couldn't sustain the grafts implanted by Ingarden; his gifts, unfortunately, had failed to take root.

One or twice I'd attended his lectures at the Philosophical Society. But maybe because the audience in attendance here was quite advanced in years, slightly deaf, and somewhat blind, he never achieved the miraculous feats his former students had described. (An auditorium full of young students is more conducive to revelations. Moreover, the student lectures took place early in the morning, when the master magician had far greater energy at his disposal; in the evening, though, when the society lectures were

held, aging minds inevitably drift to approaching bedtime preparations.) The hall would be bursting at the seams, and only a madman
would have dared to attack the universally revered master. Ingarden's ideological opponents, the Marxists, largely ignored his lectures; they didn't bother to show up, with one exception, a Marxist
with a little more imagination than the rest, who wore a leather
jacket to set himself apart from Engels's bureaucratic acolytes in
their standard-issue gray suits. But Ingarden's followers turned out
en masse. They sat in the front rows, like apostles, and took down
all the teacher's words, which they would later make known
throughout Krakow and outlying towns. One of Husserl's terms
came under discussion after one lecture. It was a minor point, not a
key concept of phenomenology, and Ingarden said jokingly, "Husserl's coffee must not have been strong enough that day." I felt as
though I'd been present at the birth of a new, informal method of
hermeneutic criticism: "His coffee must not have been strong
enough"! How many dubious theories would collapse beneath the
weight of such an argument!

Once I saw him buy a record of Karol Szymanowski's second
violin concerto in a bookstore on the Old Market, Gebethner's
Books. And sometimes I'd see him strolling beneath the tall green
ceiling of the Planty gardens' trees.

The students worshipped Ingarden. We wanted to find out
everything about him, although in fact we knew next to nothing.
Only that he napped in his office every day after lunch, as befitted a
traditional, elderly professor of philosophy. We'd never seen his
office, and we never would (we only knew which street it was on,
and an unearthly light seemed to permeate that street). Precisely
because of this ignorance, though, we could furnish it just as we
liked in our heads, guessing where the desk (monumental, of
course!) was placed, where the bookcases stood (books in every language), where he'd put the armchair (uncommonly comfortable),

and where he'd set the sofa (green?) on which he took his sacramental siestas. It didn't matter whether we'd actually borne witness to his magnificent materializations; all of us, junior and senior students alike, were convinced that the entire city fell silent while the philosopher took his naps. His siestas stopped traffic, halted the rackety, sky-blue streetcars in their tracks; and if they didn't, they should have, since if the city persisted in living while he slept, it was living at its own risk, leading a lawless, reckless existence, like a mongrel or a weed.

I have to confess that I've already written a book about Krakow. This was a novel, not a long one, called *Warm, Cold*. Its hero's name was Oremus; and he shared certain biographical traits and experiences with me. Not all of them; for example, his father committed suicide in the novel, leaving his widow plunged in grief and despair. It was pure fiction, a literary trick. Once, though, a friend from Warsaw who'd read the novel asked me how my mother was holding up—this was many years ago, sometime in the seventies—without so much as mentioning my father. He was startled when I brought this up: What on earth are you talking about, your father committed suicide. Well, not exactly. That was just a literary trick. And all the other complications occasioned by the father's death took place only in my imagination: Mr. Orzech, whose task was to comfort the widow once she'd emerged from her sorrow, was a purely fictional character.

My hero went off to study in Krakow after he'd finished high school—this all sticks pretty closely to my life. He strolls through Krakow, observing its apartment buildings ringed with balconies— from the outside, almost always from the outside. He's obsessed with these buildings, he sees mysterious qualities in them, imagining, no doubt mistakenly, the rich, secret intellectual life that they must harbor. At times he catches sight, from the street, of an oblique slice of someone's apartment (this isn't Holland, where apartments are put on display, illuminated in such a way that every passerby can check what's going on inside): bookshelves, perhaps the silhouette of someone's head, a lamp's yellow light, a picture on the wall, some flowers. My hero is a bit homeless—just as I was during my studies—and for this reason overrates the lamps and their warm, yellow, cozy light, which weren't in fact all that attractive. He wants to penetrate the city's heart; like any young man who's read too much Balzac, he wants to take the town by storm. But he can't, it's too early or too late. Marrying a wealthy young lady wouldn't do the trick—and how would you go about locating such a young lady in this sorry country anyway? To make things worse, he's been given a certain reckless gift, some inner life, a bit of talent.

It was a bildungsroman, as the scholars say; my hero, naïvely or not, sought the truth. There's one scene that takes place at the university; some cynical professor or lecturer dismisses any notion of the truth. My hero stands up for the truth, though; back to the wall, he answers that he recognizes the truth by the feeling of warmth inside his head.

But this doesn't save him in the end. He perishes, spiritually at any rate, in the abyss of a petty, bureaucratic totalitarianism. He begins to serve the system, however indirectly, and loses his soul. One of my friends was outraged: You're glorifying the system, your book helps the system destroy people! But that wasn't what I was after; the ending was meant to be satiric, negative, and I hope that most of my readers caught this. The novel's hero turns out as I myself might have ended; he becomes what anyone must become once the dry angel of conscience has deserted him.

The Louvre is full of paintings by masters of different schools—
Italian, Dutch, Spanish. And crowds of Italians, Spaniards, Dutch-
men fill the Louvre's halls with faces that mirror those in the
paintings.

One day a Nazi flag appeared on the walls of Wawel Castle. They
were shooting a film.

Wojtek Pszoniak was three years older than I was. So when we were
kids we belonged, in effect, to two different generations. He lived
on the second floor of the apartment house on Arkonska Street, and
I lived on the third. His family had also come to Gliwice from
Lwow, from the sacred city to wretched, industrial Gliwice. Supposedly, he once said something nasty to my sister. My mother
decided he was no good, and wouldn't let us play with him. He was
an active, wiry, redheaded little kid. I didn't play with him, but I followed his doings closely. He had the most compelling personality
of any child on Arkonska Street. Of course, it wasn't much of a
street, but still every building had its children, and each child had a
personality, though it might be as microscopic as a poppy seed.

Wojtek was the subject of a pedagogical experiment; he
dropped out of school early on. I remember once seeing him march
at the head of a military parade, beating a drum. I saw this from the
balcony of our apartment (we'd moved to a different building on
the same street by then). Look, my mother said, he'll never amount
to anything, he's just an army drummer. Later he piloted gliders.
He started out as though he belonged to an entirely different generation, a generation of tumultuous writers and brawlers, disciples

of the philosopher from Basel, who couldn't abide the relentless
quiet of a writer's study and sought adventure in wars, revolutions,
and rebellions. He made friends with Tadeusz Rozewicz in Gliwice.

He also became an actor in Gliwice's student theater—as if the
explosive force contained within him had finally found an outlet on
the stage. I actually saw him onstage only in Krakow, first in
Swinarski's production of *A Midsummer Night's Dream*, and then in
various other roles, including his performance in the adaptation of
Dostoevsky's *The Possessed* directed by Andrzej Wajda. He was Puck
in *A Midsummer Night's Dream*, and he was wonderful, full of the
amazing energy I recalled from years ago. It had taken on new forms,
though; he raced around, played seesaw, mocked himself, the theater,
his own red shock of hair. He played the young Verkhovensky in *The
Possessed*, and he paced the stage just the way that Lenin must have
strode through Zurich's narrow streets (or rather, just as Lenin
wished he'd strode, since in reality he probably walked more like a
bookkeeper). He was terrifying; he managed to capture the horror of
revolution, the pure thirst for destruction. He unmasked the menace
contained in an energy that fizzed like champagne, an energy
directed toward an unfamiliar, bloody future, one that could not be
appeased by what actually exists—or by what is no more. The character of the young Verkhovensky was modeled, as we know, upon
Nechayev, an exceptionally cruel and duplicitous revolutionary, a
man for whom the murder of a fellow conspirator was simply a matter of common sense: it cemented the group. I should add that Pszoniak's Verkhovensky was also a very ordinary young man who might
easily have had—why not?—a pimple on his nose. This banality was
beautifully spliced to the dynamite of his collusions and plots.

And this was someone I knew from the courtyard of our building in Gliwice, the drummer who was bound to turn out badly
("he'll never amount to anything") according to the ladies of
Arkonska Street, that Greek chorus of ladies who'd come to Silesia

from Lwow and looked down their noses at the others. His transformation startled me; he'd turned into art. It was as if the kid I'd
known long ago had been completed by something else. He was
still pretty much the same boy I used to bump into back then even
though he was now nearing thirty. Physically, he was almost
unchanged, he'd been transformed from within. He had keenness
and strength; it should have been blindingly clear that he was a
born actor, any passerby should have trotted him off to drama
school on the spot. And yet he had to apply two times. He wasn't
accepted the first time out; they said he was the wrong type physically. And in one sense they were right: he couldn't have played the
moony lover, the athlete wielding his mighty sword. He wasn't a
lover, he was Verkhovensky, Puck, Robespierre, someone drawn
from the realm of troubled, spiteful souls: he was the "eternal husband" of Dostoevsky's tale. (Much later, though, he played the good
Dr. Korczak in Wajda's film, and played him beautifully.) In Warsaw, he played Robespierre in Stanislawa Przybyszewska's *The
Death of Danton*; his narrow face looked like a guillotine's blade.
And he was a Jewish industrialist in Wajda's *Promised Land.*

He'd been completed by something we didn't know about back
on Arkonska Street, by something invisible. It's as if all of us—
all?—must be completed by something that isn't us yet but might
become us. We aren't all able to find our proper complement, but
Pszoniak was remarkably successful: he sniffed out the right thing
with lightning speed. His parts expanded him, he grew through his
roles, he grew by way of Shakespeare, Dostoevsky, Stanislawa Przybyszewska, Reymont. But he also did these distant authors a great
service: he offered them his effervescent youth. He aided the dead.
Dead writers need young actors with their explosive energy; otherwise they fall prey to the grave's silence. Once upon a time the
fairest youths and maidens were sacrificed each year to sate the
gods; dead writers require this now.

He gave them his surplus of life; he woke them from sleep, from drowsy immortality, he entered into another beauty, and thus disciplined his own unruly appetites. He was Fortune's favorite; fate smiled on him.

I watched him from the theater's dark hall, one of several hundred viewers, a young poet, unsure of his identity. I hadn't yet been completed by that enigmatic, extra something. (What could it be? Style? Self-possession? Agitation?) I envied the speed with which Wojtek transformed himself into one or another figure drawn from some vast waxworks. Like a steed loosed from his fetters, the young Verkhovensky terrorized Russia, Europe. And this was my childhood friend, adept at the metamorphoses of which I dreamed. He became Puck, set up shop in Shakespeare's imagination and lent him a hand, helped to raise Dostoevsky from the dead.

Streets steamed after the rain. Umbrellas steamed too. Summer. Some old man made anti-government speeches, but no one cared, not even the secret police, who were usually so quick to defend their ambiguous privileges. Dog owners started turning up around dusk in the city's squares and parks. Dog owners are a polytheistic sect, since each worships only one small deity, his own pet. It's a genuine cult, with its own rituals. It's considered self-evident that owners always walk their pets at sunset. They especially liked the Common's vast expanse; the Common opened its extensive territories, brought fresh air from the cosmos almost to the city's center, to the Old Market. A triangular meadow. The Bois de Boulogne intrudes on the body of Paris; but Paris is an erotic city and the Bois de Boulogne thus resembles the tuft of hair beneath a woman's belly. Krakow is completely different, a city full of hypocrisy or restraint (or patience). The Common is vacant, the grass makes no assumptions. Each evening dogs busily surveyed—and still survey—the fields by tracing even, sweeping circles, as if drawing rings within the Common's triangle were their most pressing occupation.

What is completion? A small-scale model of transcendence given to someone who without this gift would just have been himself. And being yourself alone just isn't enough. How dull to be nothing but yourself!

The days when I can't write at all stay mute forever. On such days I can defend neither poetry nor prose. At best the steady working of my heart.

This is what Goethe wrote on parting with Maria Szymanowska: "I refuse to regard remembrance the way that the rest of you usually do, as a very clumsy form of self-expression. When something great, serious, beautiful happens to us, there's no need to pursue it afterward in memory; rather this event must from the outset merge with our innermost being, meld with it, shape within us a new and better 'I,' and live inside us eternally, co-creating our selves into the future.

"There is no past that we should yearn for. Only the eternally new truly exists, which takes its shape from those elements of the past that continue to grow. True yearning must be creative, must give birth to new and better things. And—returning to Maria Szymanowska—haven't we experienced this within ourselves just now? Don't we sense that this enchanting, noble creature who wants to leave us now has changed us inwardly, restored us, made us larger, better? No, she won't be able to abandon us completely, she dwells inside our hearts, she lives within us. Oh, even if she wished to abandon me completely, still I will keep her forever within me."

"Good Lord, these Germans are ugly," says N., glancing at the conductor's picture on the record cover.

"This isn't possible," a woman said on the express train to Wroclaw as the train stood for half an hour in a field.

The effect of poetry is difficult to define; sometimes a great poem suddenly opens a new expanse before us, almost literally, as though someone had carved a large patch out of a mountain, as though an enormous tower touching the sun had taken shape with lightning speed. For example? For example, Osip Mandelstam's "I Washed My Face in the Yard at Night":

> I washed my face in the yard at night,
> Coarse stars filled the firmament.
> A starry ray, like salt upon an ax,
> The brimming barrel freezes over.
>
> The gates are under lock and key,
> The earth is strict as conscience—

How could a foundation be found
Cleaner than the fresh canvas's truth?

In the barrel a star melts like salt,
And the frozen water blackens,
Death is cleaner, grief is saltier,
And the earth is more honest and awful.

"I washed my face in the yard at night," Mandelstam says—and
the whole earth bathed with him, cleansed itself, and stood revealed
in its terror.

In a bus once someone started holding forth, insisting—it was mid-
May—that summer was just about over. It's mid-May now, the
argument ran, June is always over before you know it, then July's
gone by, next it's August, then suddenly you've got September and
the weather's getting cold!

It's not time we lack, but concentration.

Aunt B. hadn't had an easy life; she was Jewish, but she fell in love
with a Gentile, so her family cut her off. And it took a long time
for the family of her fiancé, later her husband, to accept her, since
she was Jewish. For many years she dwelled not on the terra firma
of a stable, middle-class existence but on the narrow dike dividing
two communities. And she yearned for something completely dif-

ferent. She wanted to be ordinary, to have a house, like everyone else. She just wanted a regular life, guests for dinner, a few jokes. It was precisely for this reason that Aunt B. struggled her whole life to be *comme il faut* in her conduct and conversation, a typical member of a cultured Polish family. In Lwow she belonged to the Society for Ladies of the House. Unfortunately, this society ceased to exist after the war; she would have been its mainstay otherwise.

In Communist Poland, she took part in the elections—an obvious farce—well into her old age. I was fanatically caught up in the opposition at the time, and tried to persuade her by way of ironclad arguments. But in her case participation in these pseudo-elections was due to a type of conformity that lay far beyond my comprehension. It was the poignant conformity of a person who dreaded the chilly emptiness of social anathema. Two different forms of censure threatened her: one was Jewish, while the other stemmed from the Polish Catholic intelligentsia. (By the time I knew her, of course, only this last danger still existed, and even it had been thoroughly averted.) There was no place for her; if these two contradictory dangers had actually materialized, she would have perished. Her conformity wasn't petty, as such things usually are; this wasn't the routine defense of a comfortable, privileged existence. Aunt B.'s conformity verged on the heroic. It didn't concern creature comforts; it was rather a desperate defense of her own existence and that of her cherished, helpless husband, my elegant uncle Jozef, at least while he lived. (They were childless, and to this day I don't know if this was because they couldn't have children or because they had both decided that they had no right to perpetuate their own threatened identity and thus expand their embattled no-man's-land.)

She survived the war and occupation in a village outside Tarnow; she rarely spoke of this. It was a taboo, one of many. If she recalled her life in the village at all—as a Jew, she was hiding from

both Nazis and Polish informers at a time when her life was in lit-
eral danger every day—it was only as a prolonged vacation, an
extended stay in the country. And even then she only mentioned
Uncle Jozef: "You know, he would play cards for days on end while
we were living in the country." So the picture she painted of their
village life, those many years in hiding, was perfectly idyllic: holidays, cards, pleasant company, a never-ending cruise through the
Mediterranean aboard a luxury liner.

Many years after Uncle Jozef's death, during the last year of her
own life, I finally asked her about Uncle Jozef: did he talk much,
what were his hobbies, did he like to read, and so on. She talked
about him in the present tense: "Oh, he's always sitting with his bits
of paper. Yes, he likes reading, but he doesn't have much time for it.
He's always checking those slips from the bank." Then I understood that Uncle Jozef was immortal, that he was sitting right
beside us, poking through his papers.

She was a person from the peripheries—her family must have
been orthodox if their daughter's apostasy provoked such a radical reaction—who did everything in her power to look as though
she came from the very heart of society. She was exhaustingly
proper.

She never mentioned her Jewish family. One didn't speak of it; it
wasn't done. One brought up only mentionable topics: ill health,
long-past trips to Vienna, dinner parties, family, or, strictly speaking, Uncle Jozef's family. From her own family, only one person
still existed in her small talk: a sister, a doctor who lived in
Zakopane and occasionally came to Krakow.

I can't say that her talk was engaging. She wasn't a person
with original convictions, she never came up with any deep or
startling ideas, she never read exciting books. Still, I went to see
her fairly often, and not just from family obligations. I liked her,
her history intrigued me. I liked her face and her large, dark

eyes. She had a distinctive personality, she stood out among anonymities.

For a few years I lived right near her; I lived on Urzednicza Street, while her quiet little apartment was in a building on Chocimska Street (Tadeusz Kantor lived in between us, on Spokojna Street). And when I went to see her, as a student and then after the university, I saw before me someone who'd sustained a victory. She'd finally managed to escape the inhospitable dike she'd occupied earlier, and had taken up residence for good within her adopted society. She'd been accepted. The threat of social oblivion that had been her bane for so many years had vanished for good, like a bad dream. Even many years after Uncle Jozef's death, the guests at her name-day party were unquestionably *comme il faut*; as a widow she held a secure spot in cultured, refined society. And she identified herself with this society completely; perhaps she'd really forgotten, even in private, in moments of solitude, about her first family, her first identity.

Even when she grew quite old and feeble, and had to shuttle between the hospital and her own apartment, she continued to behave in a manner befitting a member of the best society: "But the riffraff they've got in those hospitals, completely unacceptable. The nurses must be illiterate! I don't even think they bathe! The people are *très simple*; or perhaps merely *simple*."

Her salient feature—which set her apart from other women of her generation and social position (that is, impoverished, but aware of their culture and merit)—was anger. Anger dwelled in her, unabating anger, like a smoldering fire. This anger was the only sign of her difference and her pride. Anger was the sign of her pride, and of the valor with which she had waged her stubborn, protracted war for survival, and for recognition of herself, her choice, her marriage, her difference. Or perhaps she'd been born with this pride; perhaps Uncle Jozef fell in love with her precisely because that inextinguishable anger had burned in her even then. And the anger that was her stigma, her sign, was unconnected to her later sufferings. I liked to imagine her as a young Jewish girl, not pretty—I don't think she'd ever been pretty—but set apart by her pride, her irrational pride. It was neither Jewish, nor gentry Polish. It was primal, unfounded; she was proud of her very being, her existence.

Her life bore a distinctive stamp. It was marked by the paradoxical fusion of intense conformism, mimicry, a carefully elaborated system of adaptive habits, on the one hand, and an angry pride, on the other, which violently negated the system that formed the steel corset of her existence. "This is utter nonsense, don't believe me, I'm not really here at all!"—or so her eyes seemed to proclaim.

Aunt B. battled entropy successfully for many years. She was already quite old and rather weak, but she still maintained that a vacation should be taken every summer. And she would leave for Szczawnica for a month or two each year. At a certain point, though, she made her way around Krakow only with difficulty, and had to abandon Szczawnica for hamlets closer to home. I can't imagine how she spent these vacations.

She lived to be nearly a hundred, and in this she was no doubt as entirely *comme il faut* as she had been when she went to the doctor for the first time upon reaching the age of ninety. She made it clear on more than one occasion that she did not entirely approve of invalids. She didn't come right out and say it, but she often commented on others' ill health or premature—to her mind—deaths in a tone that mingled sympathy with censure, as if these unfortunates were themselves to blame, as if they'd missed something, hadn't grasped some simple truth, some perfectly obvious fact. Her head never ached, she never caught cold, she didn't know the meaning of hypertension, she had no idea where her liver was or what her kidneys did.

She filled with pride whenever I complained, for example, that my head ached. She would look at me with astonishment: "So young, and already you have headaches? What next?" And when my sister's husband died, she shook her head incredulously, as if to criticize—indirectly of course—my sister's unfortunate choice. One should always select a supremely healthy spouse.

And when she herself went to the doctor for the first time, it was already too late; she made her visit only after taking a tumble on the street, when she'd already begun to weaken. It never occurred to her that she might ask him to make a house call. But right afterward she began her prolonged and painful descent into death. And death took its revenge for its sustained humiliation, for the many years of vigor and energy she'd enjoyed without recourse to doctors, for her decades of health and reason. She died terribly, divided between the hospital she hated—staffed as it was with "riffraff"—and her own room, which she no longer recognized. Death toyed with her for two years, stripping her of her sense and memory.

An improvised family council looked after her; and finally they found a way to save her from the hospital. They promised a handsome young medical student that he could have the apartment after her death, and so he moved into the kitchen, where he slept, studied, and took care of the old woman. He was so good-looking, and so full of careless, schoolboy good spirits that he scarcely noticed his patient's hopeless condition. But she would gaze at him tenderly and take his hand. He was her last love. She must have taken him for Uncle Jozef. I'm sure Uncle Jozef would have forgiven her.

Norwid wrote a scathing poem about leaders who command only "on Sundays." The philosophers of religion who, like Mircea Eliade,

focus only on the experience of the sacred, which they see as the ful-
crum of our lives, the force that organizes all the rest of our existence, are a little like these "Sunday leaders." The overwhelming
experience of the sacred is no doubt an essential element of any religion. But the week isn't made up only of Sundays; there are days
when the powerful voice of the sacred falls silent, when we must
think about ourselves, about those dear to us, about our ethical
choices, about a world that's merely ordinary, not Dionysian. And
one must find meaning and direction even in this ordinariness, one
must find the calm and courage of an ordinary life.

I went to Silesia every week or two because I had a girlfriend back
in Gliwice, where my parents lived. Blue and yellow trains traveled
regularly between Krakow and Gliwice, quivering nervously like
someone who's just quit smoking and doesn't know what to do with
his hands. In the train, especially on the way back to Krakow, I'd
prepare for classes or read "real" books. This was the phase of
Kafka, Nietzsche, and Bergson. I lapped up Kafka's dark aphorisms,
admired the young Nietzsche's audacity and style, sought to exit
the intellect's trap by way of *Creative Evolution*. I believed in intui-
tion, that enigmatic, third power; that Bergson, a French writer,
proposed this mad solution only magnified the attractions of his
thought.

I was convinced that language lies; I hadn't yet given a thought
to the language of the daily papers, that bête noire of the so-called
New Wave (the name that was later given to the poets of my generation). I was thinking of language in general. I rarely saw any con-
nection between my own life and thoughts and the black marks on
the pages of my books. Language was a traitor; it couldn't tran-
scribe thought. I don't know if what concerned me was the meta-

physical imperfection of language itself or my own personal afflic-
tion; I didn't know how to say anything.

In the winter the trains were overheated and stuffy, my neighbors' fur coats tickled my ears; hundreds of students were returning, as I was, from a weekend at home with their parents in Silesia.
In spite of the hothouse atmosphere, though, ferocious attacks of
inspiration occasionally struck me, and I'd reach for a pencil or pen
to jot down embryonic metaphors or lines of verse on the dust
jacket of my book. These lines seldom survived the train trip; after
a day or two they struck me as clumsy or banal. (Language had
betrayed me once again, I told myself . . .) Sometimes, instead of
bits of eternally unfinished poems, I'd compose some limping
aphorism, which I would proudly display to my girlfriend. I remember being particularly taken with this saying: "Phrasemongers com-
mit suicide by shooting themselves in the mouth." Lines written in
an electric train (language lies). But my girlfriend was ecstatic.

Anyone who writes, or tries to write, and plans his day around the
thought of the task that awaits him, has to grapple with two basic
problems: (1) how to get up in the morning, and (2) (if he manages
the first) how to get to sleep at night.

In times like ours, besieged by stupidity and amnesia, memory, naturally enough, is extremely precious. And poetry is often considered a kind of tribute presented to the god of memory. The elegy
thus becomes the king of poems; it not only keeps our losses from
oblivion but struggles to immortalize them, to preserve the freshness and force of what has passed. (The elegy isn't an epitaph! It's

closer to an epithalamium, since it celebrates the marriage of past and present.)

One hears less about the role of anticipation in poetry, both in its content and in the stance of the poet or reader. In a certain sense, a poem is never really finished, it's always ahead of us. The author and reader always dream of a great poem, of writing it, reading it, living it. And every elegy always conceals the hope that the miracle it celebrates, the miracle of someone's life, of some event, will come into being once again (it's come back in the poem, after all!). A poem's mystery is always ahead of us. And the author and reader will never be sated, they'll always put off that one last poem for later. We wait for death in the same way: it's both final and fearful but, who knows, perhaps joyous as well.

If memory usurped anticipation's place completely, we'd already be dead. Or we'd come to resemble those idiots who don't understand anything but can't forget anything either, not a thing, not a single quote, number, or event.

"You can't get by on poetry." Taken literally, the phrase's sense is obvious: you can't support yourself financially by writing poetry. Everyone knows this nowadays; perhaps only very young poets still refuse to acknowledge and accept this fact. But "you can't get by on poetry" can also mean something quite different. You can't get by on poetry, with poetry, in a spiritual sense as well. Poems, and particularly the short lyric poems that prevail today, have one distinctive feature: they don't last. They offer us, at best, a moment of intense experience. A volume of poetry calls to mind something like a loosely knit conglomerate of "moments," which may be quite stirring but fail to form a single entity. Or so it is commonly thought.

At the same time, observing today's readers, the passengers on suburban commuter trains and in subway cars, would seem to indicate that thick novels are the preferred genre today, and not, God forbid, short stories, for example. These may not be the novels whose titles will resound in coming centuries, but their virtue lies in their capacity to link a multitude of fleeting moments; the narrative binds together, as in a bouquet, the flowers of isolated instants. A deep, perhaps wholly unconscious, desire for synthesis prods people through this arduous reading. They yearn for synthesis, for the magical zipper that would fuse and seal their poorly knit existences.

Poems, solo fliers on the pages of a book of verse, don't appear to hold out this hope of fusion; in this they are like notes, thoughts, and aphorisms. To the inattentive reader, such snipped-up texts seem to be going nowhere.

But discontinuous texts resemble at times the segments of a curved line; at first nothing suggests consistency or wholeness. Only later does it turn out—sometimes, at least!—that these fragments are the slices of a circle, and with a bit of luck and attention one may trace the radii extending to the center.

But perhaps imagination also requires moderation, compromise— just as we ourselves do in our practical, everyday lives, where we can't get by without making certain concessions. The imagination checks itself by rejecting absolute autonomy, by resisting the kind of total divorce from reality that some of the surrealists, for example, recommended (thus outraging Simone Weil!).

It's as if two forces were at work in the imagination, one centrifugal, prone to folly, dismissing the real world, and the other, calmer, more sober—the Gypsy with eyes wide open, the Gypsy who tells fortunes but never forgets to count the take.

Benedetto Croce reminds us of the need for such concessions in a lesser-known "defense of poetry" that he presented sometime in the thirties at the invitation of Oxford University.

To look without being seen—this is the gift of early youth.

The hero of my novel from the seventies effects a shameful compromise with reality: he accepts a position in a discussion circle as a kind of "resident dialectician," whose task is to smooth over any serious disputes that threaten to erupt. At the start of such an argument, he gets up and, taking his lead from a sort of people's Hegelianism, proposes a propitiatory synthesis.

It's a satiric image, a portrait of spiritual death.

If one were to look more kindly on the hero—and thus move beyond the book itself—one might perceive in the mechanized gesture that dialectically fuses opposites an image for the hero's own helplessness in a world torn asunder. He inhabits a world in which vital, fundamental values have worn as thin as those banknotes, torn in half, that spies who belong to the same network use to recognize one another. The tradition of the Enlightenment, for example, offers him a bit of freedom, some regard for reason, but not much by way of poetry and the divine. In the domain where divinity and poetry abound, though, he may also encounter the stern visage of authority, and not only in the spiritual realm, as one might expect, but also in the social sphere. And this would be more than he could bear. My hero is clearly an example of humdrum opportunism—but one might also see him as my own caricature, a person stranded in a world of confused, shopworn, unequally divided values. And this person seeks out synthesis, even if he goes about it in exactly the wrong way.

How does one look for synthesis properly, not mechanically, like an epigone, but "organically," honestly? If I knew, I'd come right out and say it . . . But one must try.

Who were we back then? Twenty years later, the image is hazy, far from clear. And human personality, after all, is always something mysterious, elusive, with ill-defined boundaries. But still all these people lived, knew suffering and inflicted suffering—like swimmers, at night, in a dark lake, beneath the cupola of a cloudy sky. You hear cries: is it pain or rapture?

The second trip was longer. I traveled for many hours by bus to Krynica, where I was to repeat my lecture on "Ethics and Morality" in a local rest home. If I remember rightly, it was on the same day that Gomulka, the dictator of the day, gave a speech at the Party Congress. If I'm not mistaken, this was a speech famous for its great length; it lasted seven hours, during which the people's leader covered every sphere of human life. Since the Party controlled everything, it was obliged to report on its activities in various domains: construction, the engineering industry, agriculture, the production of beets and strawberries, the distribution of paper clips, the condition of workers' cafeterias, the taste of borsch in state-run restaurants, the social status of shoemakers, the witticisms of tailors, the quality of apples, pencils and erasers, ink, men's and women's underwear, the situation of actors, journalists, accountants, miners, civil and military pilots. There was something about this colossal catalogue of world poetry that took one's breath away. What unaccountable ambition, this desire to master each pebble on the mountain path, each toad in the village pond, each mosquito!

This dreary dictator yearned to be a new Mickiewicz, to place all reality beneath his pedantic control. Unfortunately, he wasn't up to the task: only a great poet, the greatest of all poets, could embrace this vast terrain with his eagle eye. Poland, it is true, wasn't all that large, but like an old cupboard, it held vast quantities of drawers, which concealed immeasurable treasures: nicked swords, engagement rings, sepia photographs, silver pencils, books, and human intellects, ideas, both original and borrowed, fresh and stale.

It was an unusually absorbing enterprise, drawing up an exhaustive inventory of both the seen and the unseen worlds, but the task, as I've said, proved to be beyond the capacities of our balding dictator.

I have no idea why the bus driver switched on the radio. I doubt that he was a great fan of Gomulka's: these were few and far between. And he wasn't governed by fear, since at that point no one was ordering bus drivers to follow Party speeches. Either he was just addicted to the radio and listened to anything that came on, or else his intentions were ironic, parodistic. This last seems likeliest to me.

Whatever his reason, the outcome was extraordinary. The crude, monotonous voice oozed from the speaker, systematically listing every realm of human existence while the bus, steeped in the provincial darkness of an autumn day, was truly, literally grounded in the material world, in the geographical slapdash of Krakow's peripheries. As it passed from one village to the next, from one town to another, it inadvertently gave the lie to the aging tyrant's claims. It wasn't the bus driver who mocked our leader (assuming that's what he was after). It was the dirty sidewalks and cramped streets of these ugly little towns, even the very darkness of early evening, the damp, gray darkness infused with the odor of gasoline and the smell of the passengers' cheap jackets.

Through the windows I glimpsed the blurred contours of telephone poles and trees, the frantic flickering of neon lights framed
by halos of grimy haze, the empty windows of sorry shops, the silhouettes of drunken men who swayed on the unstable ground.
Sometimes a little mutt would run alongside the bus for a long-
drawn moment, barking ferociously. An aging bicyclist ascended
the hill uncertainly (he was drunk too). The air was damp and
seemed to dissolve the houses' outlines. Lamps trembled anxiously,
as if fearing that the current might go out at any moment, that the
dark would triumph.

Sometimes I think my humble aunts and modest uncles, who didn't
write books or paint pictures, were nonetheless—in some mute and
moving way—true heroes of the everyday. The curses of our age
left them untouched: they didn't possess an ounce of fanaticism;
Fascism, to say nothing of Hitlerism, had absolutely no lure for
them; they maintained a hostile indifference to Communism. They
survived the persecutions of the Nazi occupation and of Stalinism.
They were skeptical, seasoned radio listeners and readers of newspapers; they never placed their faith in the topmost layer of the text,
and conducted penetrating exegeses of political coverage. They
knew that small pockets of life were still relatively free, and had to
be protected.

They lived simply, but not in poverty. They didn't take exotic
vacations; a trip to Zakopane or the seashore was a great event,
requiring extensive preparations. They wore clean shirts, although
a broken button and a collar frayed from zealous usage might peek
from beneath a woolen sweater.

They were caught up in the quotidian, or rather in defending
the quotidian from the attacks of a fanaticism embedded in histori-

cal routine. They weren't thinkers or artists, they didn't have anything radically new to offer the world. They were passive by nature,
absorbed in protecting their families, driven into a deeply defensive
position.

I see that only now, many years later. Back then I visited their
cramped apartments more from a sense of family obligation than
from genuine sympathy or desire. (Hardly anyone had a phone
then, so visits were generally unannounced.) It's true that I yearned
at times for a homelike atmosphere, which came close to a chemical
formula: kilims on the walls, a few watercolors and oil paintings
depicting another, now-vanished home (homeliness consisted
chiefly of mourning homes that no longer existed), plus tea in a
glass or cup. To this was added warmth, perhaps even goodness.

Any reader of Paul Valéry's poems and essays is intrigued by that
famous night in Genoa, between the fourth and fifth of October
1892 (a fierce storm raged over the city, and tradition was thus sat-
isfied on this score at any rate). The poet was visiting his Italian
relations, who lived near Salita San Francesco, in the heart of old
Genoa. Valéry himself called this his internal coup d'etat. European
culture has known other such nights, moments of spiritual crisis.
Who can forget Pascal's night and the flame that burned in it! But
the night in Genoa was different. That night a flame was extinguished. It was a critical night, a night of criticism, a night when
Valéry destroyed all his previous idols with one exception: the idol
of the intellect. Up until now, this feverish young poet had strode
through the clouds of fantasy, poring over the Symbolists, worship-
ping the hazy divinities of poetry, and not just poetry. But before
the dawn of October fifth he is reborn as a sober, acutely intelligent
writer who will henceforth suspect all stirrings of the soul that can't

be rationally explained. He will never again submit to inspiration, he will exalt craft and the calm, clear gaze above all transports of ecstasy or emotion.

If I were a historian of culture, I'd call attention to that night, a night when one of the age's greatest writers realized that the flame had died. The way to the twentieth century now lay open.

Afghan rugs. In the 1980s, Afghan rugs, which had drawn their designs from an age-old tradition, developed new patterns: helicopters and tanks.

I too was once a minimalist. For a time I placed my faith in some of Karl Marx's theses, I suspected all would-be higher meanings. One must exercise restraint, I told myself, one shouldn't give way to exaltation (even though I yearned at the same time for the return of those ecstatic moments I had known). The world is spartan and sober, nothing takes place without permission, there's no excess. I liked Flaubert's late writings, I loved the sardonic *Bouvard and Pécuchet*, the spiteful *Dictionary of Received Ideas*; I liked La Rochefoucauld, I was drawn by his dry, ironic style, his cynical elegance. I didn't yet know how to open myself to the whole; I still don't know.

I'm always surprised when I read or hear that in "our culture" the body is absent, neglected, slighted, shunned; people I respect, admire, sometimes even friends, feel compelled to defend this mistreated body in conversation and in print. Yet even as we speak athletes run circles around us, breathing heavily; sports are the masses' greatest passion; and the skin of passersby in the great, wealthy cities of the West is fresher than it's ever been, elastic, rosy, faintly flushed and slightly tanned, but not too much, we know that isn't healthy. Sex has finally achieved its hard-earned celebrity status, and any writer who omits descriptions of the sex act stands accused of prudery. Perhaps at some future point it will simply be forbidden to publish works that don't contain detailed depictions of copulation. The soul, on the other hand, is slowly dying, genuinely forgotten. Not the word "soul" itself—that wouldn't be such a loss, we've got other words—but the question of spirituality, the question of individuality opposing the world, questions that shouldn't be the domain of psychoanalysis alone.

Perhaps my uncles and aunts actually were poets of kindness, poets of the quotidian—but they were so mute, so timid! An abyss divided them from active, acknowledged poets. The true poet of this century worked somewhere up above them, in arctic silence—the indefatigable, invisible black poet of this age, an ironist, a skeptic, a horseman bathed in the waning light of day, arrogant and unhappy.

The piano's uninterrupted progress in *The Well-Tempered Clavier*: cuneiform scripts, which we can penetrate from time to time.

You shouldn't assume that this era—say, the early seventies—was unremittingly gloomy. When I look over my scattered notes from those years, I often find traces of the strange, schoolboy merriment that prevailed at various gatherings and meetings—giggling, nudges, muttered jokes, outbursts of wild laughter. Children left to their own devices—the parents had stepped out.

Professor Leszczynski directed my master's thesis in philosophy; he was always in the same green coat, and almost always in the same mood, depressed and muted. Like Szuman, he'd known Witkacy well, they'd been close friends. Sometimes our university seemed sown with Witkacy's former friends, as if the tail of his marvelous, chaotic comet had shattered over the Collegium Novum.

And to think that these mournful old men, who remembered better days, were forced to take on various young dunces, the insolent chairmen of the countless Party committees that clung like leeches to every possible social and scholarly body. They had to answer the spiteful queries of meddlesome secretaries and fill out scores of intrusive questionnaires.

Something in him had died. Perhaps this was the horror that followed him from Auschwitz (I'd forgotten that he hadn't been in Auschwitz!), or maybe it was his fear of the new regime's secret police. He most likely belonged to that rare species of people so delicate that they can't adapt to dark ages, to Hitlerism, to Stalinism. He was dead; in some sense he'd committed suicide. He'd killed the part of the personality that grows, yearns, bursts with laughter. Gaunt, hunched, anemic, he walked the streets of Krakow's Latin quarter.

I wrote my master's thesis with him, but as far as I recall, he scarcely helped me at all, I don't think we even met once to discuss the obstacles I might encounter. He was indifferent. He was dead inside, after all. I still liked and respected him, though. He embodied the Stoic ideal, he'd become a wise man, immune to the great world's temptations. But of course he paid for this with his boundless sadness.

I committed a minor faux pas when after my defense I gave way to a natural impulse and automatically said, "Thank you for all your help." But he hadn't helped me. He didn't say anything, perhaps he cleared his throat. He may have thought I was being sarcastic. But it wasn't sarcasm, just thoughtlessness, or maybe even a desire to show my regard for him, my respect for his symbolic essence, since his empirical form couldn't, didn't want to appear within the university's walls.

It was clumsy—but I think I suffered more than he did. I was tortured by the thought that I'd caused him pain, an old, defenseless professor who'd outlived himself.

Later in the seventies the opposition started up in full force, and I played some part in it. I attended, among other things, the private—hence conspiratorial—seminars in Pawel Kloczowski's microscopic apartment on Pawlikowski Street. At one of these meetings, Miroslaw Dzielski remarked that in the nineteenth century the chief aim of Polish intellectual activity was to find an answer to this question: How to nail the Russians. The senior historian, Professor Wereszycki, was hard of hearing. "How to what?" he asked.

"Nail them, Professor Wereszycki."

At dusk the solid blocks of buildings and churches began to soften and dissolve. The shadows and half-shadows that had dozed all day in the entryways of apartment houses emerged from their hiding places and assumed command over the gray town. The city fell to pieces: the vigorous, self-assured substance that had gathered courage from the afternoon sun gave way to cowardly, uncertain shades. Sometimes it seemed that at this precise moment I would suddenly catch sight of solitary, mournful men feverishly scribbling in their notebooks in certain spots around Krakow: on the outskirts of the Common, in the Planty gardens, by the Vistula, in the narrow streets around the Market Square. These were the dusk-writers (*crepuscolari*, twilighters!), for whom the transition from sunny, hard matter to an oblique, suspect substance, soft as a film of ice over a thawing pond in March, constituted a major, longed-for event. The endless movement of disintegration drew them more powerfully than the endless movement of accumulation.

We knew the poetry of our precursors, we'd read the great European poets. But we weren't particularly well educated. We were a group of ill-taught poets in black sweaters and jackets dusted with the obligatory offering of dandruff, a group of poets who had yet to write anything worth reading, who still didn't know how to write, mad with ambition and hormones, not overly courageous, still unaware of how much courage we would need. And we'd chosen a hard road for ourselves, the road of young people seeking artistic expression. A bunch of twenty-year-old know-nothings formed the poetic movement NOW. The name was supposed to be a manifesto. But it wasn't entirely clear what sort of manifesto we had in mind, living as we did in this venerable medieval town, which, like an aged patient in the first stages of Alzheimer's, could scarcely recall its glorious past, its Copernicus, its Faust, its Wyspianski. The name NOW suggested something radically modern; it implied that this gang of young poets in black sweaters had achieved direct

access to the present day. Perhaps it involved some mystical in-
tuition, a conviction that there exists some glowing node of pres-
entness, a certain almost ungraspable "something," a radiant
"something" about which we knew only that it had eluded other
poets and writers in the most hopeless, catastrophic fashion. In any
case, the conviction that shaped our program was—typically
enough for a group of young artists—that everything still remained
to be done. So much time had been lost, two thousand years had
passed in vain . . .

These young people who formed a poetic movement: like blind
kittens. Younger than themselves, with unawakened talents, impa-
tient, yearning to accelerate their artistic development at any cost,
expecting help and sympathy from their peers. The sympathy was
no problem, but help was a different matter: how do you help artists
who still don't have a clue? And what help can you give in the arts?

One of the chief values the poetic movement held for me was its
propensity for energetic action, since I had a tendency to put off
actual writing for later. I'd long since wanted to become a "writer"
and trusted that "something" (not the same "something," though,
that shaped the group's philosophy) in the depths of my being was
readying itself for that great task.

A poetic movement—especially a movement bearing the name
NOW!—offered me the bitter bread of urgency, of contemporane-
ity. It ripped me from the lovely sphere in which time doesn't
count, where I could read Norwid one day and Kafka the next, as if
the real, historical worlds in which they lived were completely
extraneous. It tore me from my leisurely reading, from my cozy
infinity, very like the ancient *otium*, from a paradise of literature
resembling some boundless armchair where I could comfortably,
passively, blissfully spend the next few decades. It was a descent
from the clouds, a departure from the land of dreams, a brutal
encounter with the ugliness of the present. The contrast couldn't

have been greater, the contrast between reading for pleasure, those blessed moments when the imagination, like an Oriental merchant extolling his Persian carpets, unfurls its charms, and the "now" that we announced. For this "now" was uncommonly ugly: a graceless moment in an ugly country conquered by Moscow and sentenced to mediocrity in virtually every domain.

This vast contrast was intoxicating! There was something perversely exhilarating in giving up the pleasures of the imagination and replacing them with the harsh facts of an actual country (only Krakow's charms could reconcile this contradiction). It was as if someone had wakened from a cherished dream to find himself in a prison cell. After his initial shock, he had struggled to lift his spirits and praise the brutal reality of his situation, trying to convince himself—and others!—that this reality was far better than his dream. All the while, though, he waits in the depths of his soul for that moment, temporarily postponed, when he can fall asleep again.

I soon became a propagandist, an ideologue arguing in behalf of this unattractive "now." Exiled from the paradise of imagination, where music mingled with poetry and painting, I proclaimed the primacy of "obligation" over pleasure, sobriety over reverie, society over the solitary reader and poet, history over the timelessness of artistic concentration, the concrete over the symbolic. And amazingly enough, a program closer to self-flagellation than to art began at some point to attract the attention of a public that would no doubt have remained entirely indifferent if I had stayed true to my leisurely, "eternal" dreams. (Only many years later did I return to my first enchantments and try to reconcile—if such a thing can be done—my early, immature imaginings and ideals with the chief ideas inspired by our notion of "now.")

We went on joint excursions via overheated trains to group readings, and returned en masse late at night, or stayed overnight in dorms. Trips to villages, setting up programs, strolling by the river late at night; fights, ferocious battles, and short-lived reconciliations; the moments in cafés when cigarette smoke stifled thought.

The poets of NOW perform in the club Under the Salamanders. They read poems assailing an indifferent city. Some of their more mature auditors look on ironically. A bored, tired cluster of regulars sit at the bar, dancers preoccupied with their own biological being, the task of continuing the species. Dusk falls on the Old Market. A stray bat flaps past a streetlight just where the larynx of Grodzka Street opens. These young poets still don't know that words mean more than one might think, that they can have unexpected consequences and may lead, over time, to difficult decisions. Passerby, inform the Muses . . .

Helmut Kajzar died in 1982 at the age, I think, of forty-one. He died of cancer. He was a gifted director and playwright. He was my friend. He was several years older than I was, and outstripped me in everything, in reading, in foreign travel, in his knowledge of theater and film. He was friends with Tadeusz Rozewicz and kept me posted on that angry poet. He visited me several times in the seventies, in my "own" Krakow apartment on Chrobry Street. He'd be coming home from London or Munich, he'd bought some inexpensive clothes abroad, he'd read the avant-garde authors, chiefly German, he breathed novelty and fashion. He had an engaging face and an attractive voice, and there was something appealingly frail and kind about him. He came from a Protestant family near Cieszyn, on the borders of Poland, where Catholics were the minority. He lived in Warsaw, in the heart of the city and the nation, but he bore some trace of his provincial origins, he never ceased to be a bit different, Protestant, evangelical. I liked him so much. His life was so short—and now he's gone.

The absolute cannot appear in pure and untainted form. It must cloak itself in the profane, in relativism, even in ambition or pride. Attacks on priests and poets—you can understand their ferocity from a different perspective—are beside the point.

I didn't often go to another club, the Cellar Under the Rams. I admired that splendid, famous cabaret, the pride of Krakow with its incomparably gifted artists, only from a distance. You didn't actually have to attend the shows in order to know the repertoire, the concepts, the tricks, the jokes. The cabaret and its irony permeated Krakow. New jokes would make the rounds through the Old Market and its environs the morning after a performance. The face of Piotr Skrzynecki, who refurbished the reputation of a certain unfortunate nineteenth-century general through his artistic efforts, was a common sight along the streets leading to the Market. The Cellar disseminated humor and poetry, in that order. The humor was to help you endure Communism; and to tell the truth, there was so much of it that the reserves would have done for a good two hundred years. That's how long we expected the Soviet empire to last back then. The poetry was intended to save us from apathy, from stony hardness, from an excess of twentieth-century humor.

The Cellar thus served oppositional purposes. But it was generally tolerated by the regime; the story went that even Premier Cyrankiewicz would turn up at shows from time to time.

The Cellar was an institution, a milieu, an affectation. Perhaps an affectation above all. At that time the greatest dream of the young people living or studying in Krakow—and some of their elders too—was to forge a bond with the Cellar. The Cellar didn't discourage this, and to make itself more accessible, it led a kind of double life. It put on its shows at night, and afterward you could make your way backstage to a tiny room besieged by crowds. During the day, though, you might glimpse these wizards of poetry and humor at the so-called Empik, a basement café. Stripped of their makeup and costumes, they looked more ordinary there.

The Cellar's slightly tipsy artists promenaded through the town, accompanied by a retinue of disciples (women trailed the gentlemen, while men followed after the ladies). Once I found myself in a café on Golebia Street that had been invaded by Wieslaw Dymny's little entourage (I got to know Dymny quite well some ten years later, in a military camp for troublemakers). I was having coffee with a classmate, who decided to introduce me, a "young poet," to the celebrated artist. But Dymny interrupted him, waved his hand, and said—Don't bother, I'll just forget.

One possible Parisian stroll: we get off the subway at Strasbourg–Saint-Denis. We set out on rue Saint-Denis and quickly turn left on rue de Cléry, which immediately splits into two, with rue Beauregard branching off from it. At the spot where the two streets part ways stands a building as thin as a razor; this is the wedge driven between the severed streets. We read the plaque that hangs on the building's narrow face: the poet André Chénier, guillotined in the thirty-second year of his life, lived here in 1793. We proceed down rue Beauregard; we turn left and then right again, onto rue des Jeûneurs. And then left again onto rue du Sentier. Here we find a plaque informing us that Mozart lived here; this was the stay in

Paris during which his mother died, the stay that produced one of his greatest piano sonatas, number 310 in the Köchel catalogue. We cross rue Réaumur, enter rue du Mail, and on the right glimpse a plaque which reveals that Liszt frequently visited the famous piano manufacturer Erard at this location.

And thus during this brief stroll we visit the sites of two tribulations and one triviality.

A day spent reading the poems and notes of Aleksander Wat—I've come back to this writer after a long interval. I was impressed by the dazzling power of a poet who was tortured by horrific pain in the last years of his life, and nonetheless managed to create his own synthetic language, an amalgam of Polish, literary jargon, and baroque chatter, combined with French and Russian borrowings. Near the end of his life, the end of his journey through the prisons and salons of the modern world—the border between prisons and salons is at times unsettlingly blurry—Aleksander Wat reminds himself continually that he's a lost soul, a failed poet, producing great pages all the while. He absorbs all his experiences; he synthesizes all his genealogies, the old and New Testaments, rabbinical readings, Polish romantics, German metaphysicians, the pain and bliss of meditation, sleep and hard labor. And still he manages to speak his own language—an exceptional achievement.

Compare French and German string quartets, he said. You'll see at once who has the stronger army.

———

A notice pinned up in our neighborhood: "Lost: one female setter, dark red. Answers to the name Utopia."

In philosophy the questions are obvious; they rest, so to speak, upon the surface. And this is what generates philosophy. But poetry and ambitious prose don't lack for fundamental questions on human nature and the nature of the world. Only the questions are deeply hidden. Woe to the writer who values beauty over truth.

"Mosquitoes don't hum the way they used to, they've gotten so quiet" (said once by M.'s mother).

"No, they've got it all wrong," a little-known young poet stubbornly repeated after hearing various theories and definitions of poetry.

So they asked him if he'd like to say a few words on the subject himself. He hemmed and hawed for a long while, but was finally persuaded by a charming lady and came up with a phrase or two on certain fortunate linguistic combinations, on the life of the spirit and nervous agitation (the shivers). Then he hesitated and said, "That's not it, I've got it wrong."

In 1992 I conducted a seminar in Houston on the subject of "The Imagination and Its Enemies." I don't remember now if I mentioned that the imagination itself may rank among its own enemies—if it loses its sense of measure, if it loses sight of the solid world that cannot be dissolved in art. But it's easier to discuss self-limiting revolutions than self-limiting imaginations.

Youth, youth. We all praise youth. Gombrowicz made it the basis of his philosophical system. Youth is synonymous with spontaneity, freedom, creative energy. I used to praise youth too—when I was young. I apparently wrote whole manifestos proclaiming the triumph of a "young literature," the "youthful gaze" (whatever that is!). What finally happened, though, was that I accumulated years, grew older; soon even fifty will be nothing but a fond memory, and I'll have to begin negotiations with sixty, the first fittings with that grim tailor who sews for us all and won't rest easy until he's seen us in that final suit, black as night.

So why did I first worship youth, and then, at that drawn-out moment when youth grows unreachably distant, fall silent? Why did I close that—not particularly original—chapter in my writing? Is it simply garden-variety conformity, the opportunism of an aging man of letters fighting for his place at the table? I hope not. Another possibility comes to mind here. Young people, and especially young writers, praise youth partly because that's their element, the only one they know. But other elements appear, we come to know pain, sex, marriage (its splendors and hardships), boredom, poverty or wealth, our mother's death. We change both inside and out. Hair grows scarce, we lose that famous youthful silhouette cherished by poets and painters. We learn other languages, visit other lands. We experience joy and bitterness, moments or even whole ages of grief and disappointment. Everything changes, slowly, day by day, year by year. We become different people, truly different. And yet amid this slow, serene, relentless catastrophe, one thing continues to amaze us: youth doesn't leave us completely.

Of course, it's not the same as it was: it's humbler, less dashing than before, and it comes in bits and pieces, not in one massive, gleaming block of gold. But it doesn't cease to exist. What can this mean? I see only one explanation: what we'd called youth wasn't really youth at all, just life. We worshipped life. We're all allowed to make mistakes; Columbus thought he'd found the way to India. Youth lingers on as long as we live, as long as we think, create, await the coming day with curiosity.

I had a weakness for people like Professor Leszczynski, forgotten, out of favor. (At the same time, though, I made dubious overtures to the other side, for example, my lecture trips to the provinces.) This is why I wrote my first master's thesis (yes, for some reason, I wrote two) under the direction of Mrs. Gierulanka, a cheerful woman, no longer young, and a former student of Ingarden's.

Her status was typical of those persons from the other shore, the humanists who hadn't sided with the new system but weren't considered serious foes. Her marginal existence was tolerated at the university, she'd been treated leniently (she hadn't been imprisoned, she wasn't out of work), but it went without saying that she had no voice in university affairs, and she would certainly never become a professor. She conducted the psychology proseminar and struggled above all to teach her students how to read philosophy texts honestly. It wasn't a question of the hermeneutics that became so fashionable some ten years later; she was concerned only with an intelligent, scrupulous understanding of the text.

She belonged among the ranks of old-style scholars along the lines of Professor Dambska or Professor Kreiner, who lectured on the nervous system for first-year psychology students. The "old-style scholars" were well educated and honest; they were incapable of lying, they had clean hands with close-trimmed nails. I don't want to idealize them; no doubt they too had their ambitions and rivalries. But the new breed of academics began their careers by entering the Party, and they chased after money and honors like snakes preying on field mice with their forked tongues twitching. Whereas the others, the representatives of the old school, were tidy and quiet, you didn't sense in them the restless yearning for success that drove the newer scholars.

I wrote a rather subversive master's thesis with her. It was as if the two of us, Mrs. G. and I, wanted to call a halt to the progress of modern psychology. Hence the subject of my thesis read as follows: "Introspection among Psychological Methods." I defended introspection! And this at a time when introspection was felt to be as much a relic as the brass spyglasses of eighteenth-century sailors that had given way in our age to radios and satellites. Introspection was like an old-fashioned, cruelly heavy flatiron, to which you added burning coals, or the first crystal radio sets from the twenties. New approaches, biological or psychoanalytic, had long since come to dominate psychology. And these approaches either scorned introspection or dismissed it out of hand.

I think it was Mrs. G. who first suggested this reactionary topic to me; we plotted together against a dreary, perfidious modernity, flat as the plains of Mazowsze. I thus expressed my opposition to psychology, my disillusion with a discipline that refused to acknowledge the soul and ruthlessly reduced human nature. I was, after all, a "young poet," and had no scholarly ambitions. Thus psychology seemed all the more soulless to me, a science that saw inspiration as the onset of pathology, not the revelation of a new reality.

Life had wearied Professor Leszczynski. But Mrs. G. was just the opposite; she was bursting with energy, and she happily conspired with me. Our audacious enterprise made her young again, it must have reminded her of the stirring travels of her student days.

An elderly lady thrust to the margins of the university and a young student more concerned with literature than science conspired in the quiet of Mrs. Gierulanka's study. Perhaps she saw me as a potential intellectual heir to the university's independent scholars; I would avenge Professor Szuman and the other non-Party academics.

She gave me piles of reading: I dived into dusty tomes of nineteenth-century psychology, I pored over authors who either had been entirely forgotten or were recalled only by the compilers of meticulous encyclopedias. But I also read the works of Husserl and Ingarden, my accomplice's patron saints; she'd been Ingarden's pupil, and he in turn had studied under Husserl. I read a few works in German (though my German was very poor back then), I laboriously trudged through endless, charmless pages laden with the ballast of weighty, compound nouns and lit only by the flickering, infrequent pocket mirrors of the vivid verbs that didn't turn up until the end of the sentence.

Mrs. G. had no idea that her co-conspirator was so untrustworthy. She knew that I wrote poems, but she no doubt thought that this was just a phase, a youthful passion that would soon burn out, giving way to other, less frivolous pursuits. Who didn't write a few sonnets early on? It's well known that Hegel tried his hand at poetry. Perhaps even Edmund Husserl and Roman Ingarden had succumbed to this weakness as young men. And other philosophers, too, whether famous or forgotten. (Heidegger, of course, but orthodox phenomenologists didn't take him seriously even without his poetry!) But they all grew out of it, the same way you get over whooping cough, or your voice changing.

A boundlessly ambitious conspiracy of two took shape in Mrs. G.'s snug office among the gray-covered books, beneath the portrait of Husserl; a dusty, nearsighted epidiascope lay neglected on the library shelf. The future of humanity itself was at stake here, not just the future of psychology. We wanted to restore introspection's former stature, to alert our future readers to the danger. If only we could make our case powerfully enough to persuade the world that it couldn't exist without introspection, to convince everyone, from the bootblack to the freighter captain to the nation's President, to make the regular introspective visits to their being's depths that would save their spirits, keep them from becoming mere blocks of wood, mute rocks! If we could pull this off, we could proceed to the next step and rehabilitate the soul, the spiritual life, in spite of modern scientific technology and the unhealthy tendencies of our unhappy era.

Our plotting wasn't political in nature; it was above politics. Our goals were far loftier, on a very nearly cosmic scale. Supported and abetted by Mrs. G., the expedition leader who remained on the surface of the water, I put on my diving suit and plunged into the murky waters of the past. I dived into the nineteenth century, into its bourgeois serenity, and discovered its university towns, the quiet workshops of its scholars. Swimming beneath time's rough, tempestuous current, I studied the writings of past psychologists, Wilhelm Wundt and other dreary German academics, for whom the superiority of introspection over all other approaches was absolutely obvious. Introspection was the reigning method; it was fundamental, indispensable.

We had moments of premature triumph. We were certain that the arguments favoring introspection were irrefutable, irresistible. You can't take a breath, experience a feeling, after all, without knowing that you breathe or feel. You can't live without sensing your life, you can't know jealousy or envy without being aware of it. If we think about something, we know that we're thinking about it; mental operations are reflexive in nature, they're not a black blur of oblivion, they're self-conscious, self-aware. All we had to do was present this clearly to the scientific establishment . . . And then the world of culture . . . Keep on, Adam, we're getting warm!

We proudly ignored Freud's observations. I think—no, actually I know—that my adviser considered Freud a charlatan, whose work didn't meet the most basic criteria of scientific integrity. Adam, these things can't be verified. You don't need Popper and his criteria for falsification. Freud was a fraud! He was a brave man, of course, he bore his illness with great courage. Unfortunately, though, as a scientist he was a total failure. We, on the other hand, were scrupulous, honest, unassuming, and sober. And we were defending the soul.

You must write as clearly as possibly, no similes or metaphors, God forbid: that would weaken our position. The language must be completely transparent, economical, efficient. We're not like those Party academics, we can't afford to be incomprehensible. Please forget about being a poet for now. There's plenty of time for that later. We have much more important matters at hand.

Gombrowicz loved philosophy, theory, he even lectured on intellectual history. Nothing remains of his own theory now. His entire life he wrote about nothing but himself, but we, his readers, who've pored over all his books and letters, have no idea who he was.

He was a great writer.

———

I defended the master's thesis. A bored committee heard my arguments and passed me with honors. But the world didn't change, the revolution we'd been expecting never came.

In March 1968 I was still a student—and I eagerly joined the ranks of the student demonstrators. I can't exactly say I was baptized under fire, but I did get my first whiff of tear gas.

After a week of street fighting, Sunday arrived, and we all laid down our arms. A typical, mild March Sunday—spring was in the air. I sat in my room in the apartment of the M. family on Urzednicza Street and typed up flyers directed to the workers of Krakow and Nowa Huta on my East German typewriter. Afterward, on Monday and Tuesday, I made the rounds of the cheap bars and restaurants where, so I thought, the working class must spend its evenings, and dropped off mountains of flyers.

I didn't, Your Honor, take part in a conspiracy, I acted on my own. At most, in collusion with a fellow student; he and I usually argued about basic philosophical principles, since he was a relativist on aesthetic issues, whereas I fiercely defended absolutist views. We decided to print up a leaflet summoning the workers to join forces with the rebellious students determined to unmask the despotism of our one-party government.

So it was Sunday, a mild day, the timid weather of early spring. Nothing was happening. Urzednicza Street was always sleepy and sluggish on Sunday. A lazy, lethargic street. My room was on the third floor; beneath its windows I caught sight of unhurried Sunday strollers, whose pace was different than on weekdays, a leisurely trochee. It was very quiet, nothing happened, if you don't count the tapping of ladies' heels. The tapping shoes of ladies dressed in their Sunday best on their way to or from the church.

It was so quiet that my typewriter's drumming seemed as though it must be audible at a distance of several kilometers. The two kinds of tapping—high heels and my typewriter—mingled from time to time. There were no other sounds; the blackbirds hadn't started singing yet. Carpenters didn't saw wood on Sundays, ironworkers didn't labor in their cramped, noisy shops. I thought that the entire city must be listening to my GDR typewriter. I churned out leaflets and counted on the support of the working class.

I now think that introspection is pure boredom—that is, if you see introspection as self-absorption, and not as attending to the voices of others, the living and the dead.

Of all the libraries I know, the worst is probably the vast library of the Centre Pompidou at the Beaubourg in Paris. It actually has quite a good collection, and it subscribes to the wonderful American principle of ready access to the stacks, which means you can roam freely among the books yourself. On the other hand, though, it calls to mind the vast waiting room of a central railroad station. Besieged by hordes of students and vagrants, it doesn't offer much by way of peace and quiet. In addition, as befits a railroad station, it's been equipped with loudspeakers, which make announcements in a very civilized voice every fifteen minutes or so: "Please look out for pickpockets. Do not leave your personal belongings unattended."

These announcements break the readers' concentration, awaken them from their reveries, from that strange space we occupy while we're absorbed in reading. Each reader glances up involuntarily, struggling to understand what's going on. But it's only pickpockets.

Yet I still like this peculiar reading room. Maybe it's a test case for the future. Huge halls and loudspeaker announcements. Concentration achieved only with the greatest of difficulty, constant interference from the staff and director. For example: Would the lady seated at Table Four please cease her ecstasies over Baudelaire and pick up something pleasanter and easier to read?

Introspection isn't boring when it's transformed into prayer. It's directed outward then, toward power. It becomes an arc linking weakness and strength.

The imagination's con game: it flirts like a beautiful woman, promising access to unheard-of treasures. You'll find fire there, amazing things, come, touch the mystery, penetrate the ineffable.

But then you open the books, the greatest books ever written, and you find only what actually is. Agamemnon squabbles with Achilles over Briseis. The empty-headed, bourgeois Madame Verdurin chatters in her drawing room, Balzac's ambitious heroes chase after money and fame. Even in Dante's *Inferno* you meet not devils but Italian ruffians.

Failed incarnation. This is the gravest reproach that can be made to poetry, as Rudolf Kassner remarked to his friend Rilke. Compared with the great novels of experience and betrayal (self-betrayal), the novels of Henry James, for example, a fair share (the best share!) of the world's great poems appear to be the work of young spirits who haven't yet experienced incarnation, who sing on life's threshold, at its dawn, when reality is measured by the stern standards taken from the darkness just preceding birth. Keats, Rimbaud, and Hofmannsthal all sing with young voices. But is this actually a reproach? Perhaps it's really praise . . .

In the latter part of the seventies I received a second education, an education in the opposition. A new era had begun, far more engaging than what had come before. Enthusiasm everywhere. Underground seminars and lectures flourished in private homes, or sometimes in churches and monasteries. Crowds gathered, for example, for the lectures in the Norbertine convent on Salwator Hill, on the banks of the Vistula. I remember the lectures of Andrzej Kijowski and Adam Michnik, the readings of Wiktor Woroszylski and Stanislaw Baranczak. I'm not sure why, but it's easier to recall (this may just be my own peculiarity) the wintertime lectures and readings. The stinging frost, the lines for streetcars, the darkness of a January street, and then the warm hall filled with the animal smell of steaming furs, the hall where, almost as at home, you find yourself safely, comfortably amid familiar faces: the contrast somehow eases the memory's patient labors. Winter, the street's black void in January or December, the frantic treble of a Trabant engine starting, the electricity of the final streetcar breaking the quiet of the peaceful neighborhood—and then on the other side of the brick walls a warm hall and the patient courage of the opposition speaker.

There were always one or two secret police cars outside the monastery, usually Fiat 125s. And the driver kept the engine running, winter and summer. Of course, the cars weren't secret at all; just the opposite, they were public displays of vigilance, they

were meant to caution citizens against rashness. The violet exhaust
fumes poisoning the air signaled the presence of a tireless observer—the state.

Countless seminars and lectures! It was a true intellectual renaissance, a gleeful resurrection. The Flying University—a crazy
university—bore no resemblance to traditional institutions of
higher education with their ponderous, neo-Gothic architecture.

All the same, in spite of its ethereal name, this university didn't
take its inspiration from the traditional sources of poetry.

When I think back on my education in the opposition, I realize
that it was directed against the imagination (though it would never
have admitted it!). This was understandable: it had first of all to
remedy our backwardness in down-to-earth fields such as political
economy, recent history, political science, law.

Distinguished, independent thinkers took charge of this education; they were aided by the efforts of students intent on their
own "self-education." One couldn't ask for better schooling. It
was completely disinterested, fueled by curiosity alone, and not
by the drive for a practical degree. Perhaps for this very reason
it exposed our chief deficiency (I mean "our" in the broadest
possible sense; I have in mind the limits of modern humanity's
knowledge generally). It exposed our lack of wisdom. There was
no unified body of knowledge. Wise men made their appearance, specialists in the Imagination; but they paid little attention
to the World and its bloody dramas. And there was, on the
other hand, no shortage of scholars who knew very nearly everything there was to know about the World—but they stumbled
across the terrain of the Imagination as awkwardly as moles
upon a meadow. And so it would remain . . . Wise men who
spoke for both the World and the Imagination never made their
way to our city.

Young people—especially young artists—have the happy capacity
to experience the innocent bliss of rapturous moments, first discoveries, the feverish first moments of joy as the world's roof lightly
rises to disclose a sliver of mystery. Innocent joy! The doors open, if
only for a moment, and the light shines forth. And we're still so
young that the rapture alone suffices; we don't yet ask about its
meaning and its place in the human community's dense fabric.
We're like the gambler who wins an enormous sum and doesn't
give a thought to what he'll do with it.

Later we grow more restless and our questions become more
pressing with every year and each new revelation: What is this rapture? What is its source? And how do we make sense of it? Rapture
itself is a gift, but we must find, or make, its meaning ourselves.
Despair is something else again. It seems to offer us—willingly,
unbidden—new explanations with every passing year.

Signing letters and manifestos directed to the rulers and then published in Western newspapers (the rulers disliked this practice
intensely): this was a fairly ambivalent business with elements of
both comedy and drama. The dramatic side of these affairs was
obvious: the letters and manifestos had some political significance
and helped, slowly but surely, to build a civic society. They woke
us from our long sleep. They exposed their signatories to a certain
amount of unpleasantness, but no one was sent to Siberia for signing a dissident letter. You could lose your job, you might forfeit
the opportunity to travel abroad or publish a book. The comic
side came up in a certain innocent vanity. So did you sign it? Of
course!

After some time I became—at least from time to time, as the
need arose—an emissary from "headquarters." I made the rounds

with a letter or manifesto, urging Krakow's cautious inhabitants to take a minuscule risk.

One of these inhabitants was a professor, I believe, at the Mining Academy and the cousin of a well-known Warsaw actress; he lived in one of the city's most elegant buildings. He threw me out when I came knocking, giving me to understand that he considered me a provocateur. It was just an excuse; he was afraid. But I got thrown out anyway.

The problem of contemporary form: it's clearly easiest to find form in mockery, diminishment, rejection. The form required to praise the world is considered too complex, too difficult, too "rhetorical." A God without properties, an amorphous God—what form can capture him?

A soft city, at dawn, when the watchtowers and prisoners sleep. A soft city, unsure of its name. The sun rises solemnly. It's quiet, the first shadows lie cautiously on the cold asphalt.

What kind of meaning does poetry express—if we compare it, say, with philosophy and history? The difference might be defined as follows: poetry deals with new meanings, fresh meanings. It calls to mind a chestnut that has fallen from the tree and lost its husk; stunningly young, pink as a scar.

The last days of May in Paris: a high-pressure front centered over the Shetlands has persisted for a week. The temperature never gets above seventy degrees, but the sun shines majestically from morning to night. Paris is ruthlessly luminous at such times. It is a northern city that pretends to be Mediterranean, that claims it can live on the streets without the benefit of thick walls and furnaces. It's full of men who simply toss a cashmere scarf over their eternal suit come winter; it never occurs to them to wear a wool coat now, they're bathing at last in the sharp light of that absolute sovereign, the sun. There's not a single cloud, the sky is a deep blue, the way it sometimes is in Texas. I go out for a walk every afternoon—it's a shame to waste the weather, the light. I get out at the Quatre Septembre metro stop, I cross the passage de Choiseul, one of those arcades that still retain their nineteenth-century appearance; it hasn't been spruced up and beautified for tourists. It's easy to imagine this arcade lit by gaslight, countless little flames quivering in the drafts and the insufferable sweet scent of gas (Céline's childhood!). But the sun is shining today and its triumphant light penetrates the gallery's glass roof.

Next I make my way through angled lanes to the Palais Royal; I cross an immense courtyard. I pass along a row of young lindens that have already begun to bloom, ecstatically, as always, sweetly, carelessly. Young bees—in the center of Paris—bob diligently among the linden blossoms. Five-year-old girls and boys play in the sand while weary mothers scrutinize their dusty bottoms as if deciding whether having children was worth the bother, was it worthwhile beginning this unending epic, an epic that will become legend only when it's too late for us to see; was it worth taking up this cosmic task whose sense is too hard to comprehend, particularly on a sunny May day that makes you feel like traveling, not sitting beside a sandbox. Dogs run in circles, as always, men in gray suits, exhausted by eight hours spent in stuffy offices, study the most recent edition of *Le Monde*, checking the dollar's value (pretty high today, around 5.8 French francs) and the price of the Eurotunnel shares.

I leave the Palais Royal, just casting an eye at the shops that sell medals and orders: the world's vanity at bargain rates. If you're in the mood you can pick up a splendid baroque Spanish decoration, to say nothing of the understated Légion d'Honneur that suits a dark jacket so well. Of course, it won't be handed to you by some President or other; it's strictly self-service here, all major credit cards accepted (capitalism takes its revenge on feudalism with such restraint, even affection). I hop across a small, engaging stretch of the rue de Rivoli and reach the Louvre; the pyramid rises before me, but I make a sharp left, cross the Cour Carrée as quickly as possible, and make my way to the Pont des Arts.

I spot two brand-new swift nests over one of the Louvre's ceremonial gates; a flock of swifts flies frantically around the gate, feeding the hidden nestlings. It must be a large family, and worried about its fate. It's not clear that the Louvre management looks favorably on families of swifts; can the birds stay, or have they tightened the regulations governing the presence of foreigners in France, do these apply to cheerful little migrant birds who consume insects meant in principle for local residents?

I reach the Pont des Arts, a wooden-planked bridge, or footbridge rather, since it's only for pedestrians. From it you get an incomparable view of Paris's heart, through which the Seine flows familiarly. Notre-Dame rises on the Ile de la Cité. Roman soldiers, in revolt, proclaimed the young scholar Julian emperor on this same island in 360; he had demonstrated unexpected military gifts in Gaul. (He doesn't succeed in changing the course of the future; he will bear the name of Julian the Apostate in history books.) Constantius II, the son of Constantine the Great, was still living at the time. Julian began his armed march against Constantius from this spot, but Constantius died shortly afterward, thus freeing the road to the throne. So began the brief, fantastic reign of the Apostate, an impassioned pagan.

Swallows fly low over the river. In my childhood we thought that low-flying swallows meant rain, but I doubt that the powerful high-pressure front over the Shetlands will allow for rain today. An invisible blackbird hides in a riverbank poplar and sings for the sheer joy of it. I sit on a bench on the Pont des Arts; I catch the swallows' shrill whistle and the blackbird's inspired trill as it rises and falls. The blackbirds will sing through the end of June before they fall silent and swallows come to dominate the air of Europe. The blackbirds don't leave, they'll just slip into the shadows, discreet and mute, their lives will consist of making nests and raising children, an ordinary bourgeois existence that lasts through the first days of spring, although you can sometimes hear their song even in the dead of winter. I'm just back from Houston, where there are neither blackbirds nor swallows, so I'm all the more moved by their friendly coexistence. I'm taken by the notion that the brisk, busy swallows, with their joyful, piercing whistle, preoccupied with hunting and the charms of lightning flight, represent the element of irony. The solemn blackbirds, on the other hand, who can spend hours on end sitting motionless on TV antennae, on chimneys, on the branches of ashes or poplars, boldly personify ecstasy.

The blackbird's song glorifies the world, whereas the swallow is a bit cynical; whistling as it hunts, it mocks the lofty ambitions of the blackbird or the nightingale. It swoops in oblique trajectories, flaunting its unerring eye as it passes within a centimeter of someone's hat, dives under a stone bridge, nearly skims the surface of a river or pond, and then soars swiftly upward to the sky. Like every ironist, the swallow also requires fuel for its irony, fuel and victims; it loves society and usually flits across the evening sky in the company of friends, in large fleets, or with its wife or sweetheart. The blackbird, on the other hand, seeks solitude to sing its song. Like the romantic wanderers in Caspar David Friedrich's paintings, blackbirds require solitary outposts, the rooftops of the highest buildings, even factory chimneys. They've acquired a taste for TV antennae recently (blackbirds have been around for millions of years, while antennae first sprouted only forty years ago), and they've accepted them completely. It often happens that a blackbird will strike up its splendid, jazzy song while four stories lower one of the building's inhabitants, guessing nothing, will be watching some dreary show, the same old evening news, his imbecilic entertainment. And all the while his antenna serves the great if ephemeral art of a blackbird with a yellow beak.

Ecstasy and irony rarely meet in the world of art. When they do, it's usually for the purposes of mutual sabotage; they struggle to diminish each other's power. Ecstasy wants to dispose of its enemy once and for all, to bury him beneath the marble of solemnity, whereas irony mocks the partisans of ecstasy. For two months, though, blackbirds and swallows meet regularly throughout Europe; they ignore one another, but they peacefully coexist, they do each other no harm; the swallow's whistle intersects the blackbird's song.

There are moments when you hear not just a solitary blackbird but an entire chorus. More than once, on waking up at daybreak, I've caught an incredibly fervent choral performance of blackbirds rising above the sleeping city. The love song of the blackbirds, declaring their shared affection and soaring to ever greater heights of expression, on the one hand; then down below, beneath the rooftops, under blankets, quilts, and cotton sheets, sleeps unwitting urban humanity, a human race stuffed with sleeping pills and sedatives, steeped in its Freudian worries, analyzing its memories, jotting down its victories and losses, defending itself against prophecies. A thick cloud of singing soars above the rooftops. The air trembles with emotion. Only the trees are listening, the trees and the walls. The blackbird's song can't be compared with art, with Bach's arias; its sense eludes us completely; and if we listen too long, it may strike us as monotonous. For all this, though, it expresses us, it expresses human beings too. It's a love song, and so it's our song, the song of those who sleep and love, or loved once upon a time. What a pity that we sleep as they sing, that we aren't there to hear it, that our ears are sunk in the pillows' warm substance.

And to think that this frenzied concert, this extraordinary concert full of passion, provoking pity and envy, takes place each day at daybreak from March to June in every European city, London, Munich, Krakow, Arezzo, Stockholm. An unheard concert aimed straight at the sky, unreviewed, unattended, unrewarded, unpaid, with egoless artists.

The poor blackbirds sang most beautifully when no one could hear them except for policemen, milkmen (back when there were still milkmen), janitors scurrying to bureaus and offices, and of course insomniacs. Who knows, perhaps the inhabitants of those cities would be slightly different, a bit more generous, transformed somehow, if they'd heard this concert, which speaks to the human heart even though it's intended in principle for the hearts of small songbirds alone.

When the concert had ended, as it always does, around sunrise, when daylight vanquishes the night's intruders, silence fell, a moment of quiet, which then quickly filled with the following sound: the carefree, silly chattering of sparrows.

———

On the other side of the Seine, right across from the Louvre, a building crowned with a cupola rises, the seat of the Académie Française.

I'm going to copy out one of my favorite poems by Kazimiera Illakowiczowna, "The Enchantress":

> I have a speaking bird, I have chattering waters,
> I have an old enchanter, you may seize him by the beard;
> I have a snake who rises on his tail among the flowers,
> I have two learned hornets, who doze upon my sleeve.

> I have a splendid starling, a hedgehog, a beetle, a frog,
> I have a wise white jackdaw, a fluffy web of feathers:
> my bird will speak to you when you least expect it,
> the mournful dragon on the floor will bathe your feet in tears.

> Your first dream in the world has found its homeland here,
> and your joy sent into exile has come to live with me,
> and if, foolish armed sentry, you come to see me too,
> I'll show you your own sleeping heart inside a tiny box.

Italy's sweetness, the sweetness of Tuscany's small towns, surrounded by tender hills: who, among fortunate travelers, has not known and loved them! Each architectural fragment, each doorknob, each marble step leads its own life. Italy is tidy and gleaming. But what do you make of the ugliness of northern cities, that northeast where I spent my childhood and boyhood and part of my adulthood, too? What do you make of those places heaped with rusty junk where railroad tracks wind like mechanical snakes, where massive, shapeless blocks of concrete grow black with age? How do you make sense of those sorry villages, whose inhabitants can't cope with the world's excess, where animals constantly transgress the line that divides them from the human realm? How do you respond to those monstrous housing projects, which may seem new but become in fact more ancient than the pyramids within the space of ten years, gaping voids, though tens of thousands dwell in them? How can you love a no-man's-land, tired homesteads falling into oblivion, how do you erase the traces of homes from your memory, the ruined fences now marked only by jungles of foul nettles?

Should you side with the serene and innocent painters of Siena, artists of the *quattrocento*, for whom even hell had a certain pastel charm, whose Satan was only make-believe? Or should you follow the artists of the North, who knew full well what ugliness was, and discerned it both in people's faces, distorted by spasms of hatred, and in the imperfect union of civilization and nature? It's no contest: you head for Italy to marvel at the brittle miracle of this talented nation. On returning, though, you must remind yourself that Europe comprises both the Latin South and the barbarous North, and this division predates Yalta and other such treacherous treaties, and the North is also divided, and I too am divided.

R.: Unfortunately, he visited only the beautiful churches.

———

That brief moment of freedom: you immediately wish to offer it to somebody who's higher up than you are.

One of those people who talk. One of those people who make speeches at church bazaars, at county fairs. One of those people who talk too much. Who can't be trusted. Greasy hair slicked back with brilliantine, large nose, thick lips. I went up to him just the same, though; I approached the cluster of listeners around him. I got close enough to hear what he was saying, but not so close as to be taken for part of his audience. Close enough to hear without listening. His voice was hushed; this was striking, since people like him usually talk at the top of their lungs. This is what he said: I love life. Life needs to be . . . Let us proclaim life, not death.

Another speaker stood some thirty feet away, a slim, good-looking man, clearly a distinguished, cultivated individual; he inspired confidence. This man praised death.

It took me a moment to make my choice. I finally joined the first group, though, without regrets. It's better, I decided, to praise life alongside an unprepossessing specimen than to sing death's praises with a more impressive sort. Snobbery has its limits.

On a certain fantastic voyage undertaken in the June of 1976: in June I'd received a notice from the army, a summons to do five and a half weeks of service. It turned out I wasn't the only one who'd gotten such an invitation. Wieslaw Dymny, Maciej Kozlowski, and Stanislaw Stabro had all been called up from Krakow. We'd been ordered to appear at the camp in Hrubieszow. We quickly realized that this wasn't just the usual military exercises but rather a preemptive strike;

the camp was intended to isolate "dubious elements." About 90 percent of our campmates were criminals, while the other 10 percent
were intellectuals. Such precautions were necessary, since the rulers
were secretly planning price hikes and they expected riots.

I took the night train. The first-class compartment also held a
young couple with a small child; an older man, a bald photographer
who held forth on the mysteries of the lenses whose polished surfaces demanded such scrupulous treatment; and finally, the most
interesting pair, a calm, slightly melancholy father, maybe forty,
and his fifteen-year-old son.

We were traveling east, toward Moscow, but also toward the
enchanted East of *A Thousand and One Nights.* Tension reigned
between the father and his son; perhaps they hadn't known each
other long. Maybe the boy's parents were divorced, and the father
and child were meeting again after a long separation.

It was a moonlit night: an enormous pink moon gazed down on
the train creeping beneath it (it was supposed to be an express train,
but clearly other restrictions applied when traveling eastward from
Krakow). Excited by the moon's vast shield and the journey at night,
the boy was describing the latest car trends to his father. And how he
talked about them! Expertly, obsessively, with passion. He clearly
pored over auto magazines; he knew the most recent Italian models
and could anticipate, on the basis of his reading, the kind of chassis
that next year's Ferraris would employ, and how British manufactur-
ers would react, and if the French had any comment. The boy's voice
revealed his painful longing for these glorious, mythical vehicles; he
could have been describing unicorns. Every so often he would turn to
his melancholy father, startled by his son's euphoria, and ask, "Would
you get this car if you had the money? Well, would you?"

"Sure, sure," his father would answer with a touch of scorn, trying to soothe his agitated son. And each time he would try, in vain,
to get his son's mind off sports cars by pointing out blurry images

from the night world that lay outside the window. Look, what a tall forest. Pines, beautiful, proud pines, like ships' masts. Look at the moon, I haven't seen a moon that size in ages. Look, we're getting close to some big city.

But this had no effect on the excited boy. In a dramatic whisper—he couldn't talk out loud, since the other passengers were sleeping (I was awake)—he kept asking his exhausted father: Would you buy this one? This model? A Ferrari or a Jaguar? Which color, red or white? Would you get this one if you had the money? Sure, of course, I'd get it, but look, the stars are shining, look at the forest, the world.

As I read the bitter, ironic, modern writers, I ask myself: Why do we keep turning back to Nietzsche? There's no doubt that they are Nietzsche's offspring; they're entranced by that great stylist, that splendid saboteur. And I ask myself: Apart from anxiety, apart from ironic, inspired sorrow, what have they got on their side? Since only a child would argue that on the one hand we have profound, witty, mocking geniuses, and on the other, relentless routine, mediocrity, the quotidian with its gray suits and dull poets, the dreariness of orthodoxy and parliaments, the monotony of academic painters, clergymen with professionally pitched voices, churches, offices, banks, the international corporations that fund obedient professors who sing the praises of virtue, the family, and the balanced checkbook. No, the situation is far more complex. On this side, too, you find despair in search of fire, clarity, affirmation, despair seeking expression and finding it, if at all, only at great cost. But after all, this isn't a speech-and-debate competition!

The New Wave was a hybrid creature, a historical-artistic alloy, a metal combining collective emotions with individual imaginings, dreams, and talents. I have a strongly mixed reaction to this hybrid. On the one hand, the New Wave has nothing to do with me. It's as remote as the scraps of my first-communion suit that may still be out there somewhere in the cosmos, as the atoms of the white candle that I clasped so vertically and proudly in my palms while I posed for my portrait, a chubby-cheeked child against the backdrop of a bedsheet draped in Mrs. Kolmer's garden. I don't say this out of anger, I'm not speaking from resentment or regret, I'm not embittered, I'm not set-tling scores, I'm not moved by envy or despair (at least, I hope not). It's simply indifference toward a burnt-out form, toward a shape that hardened long ago: indifference and boredom. To write the history of one's own literary adventures—what could be more pretentious?

But the New Wave is a part of my life, just like the once-famous soccer match between Poland and the U.S.S.R. at the stadium in Chorzow, like March 1968, like the moments spent at good cabaret shows, like waiting for the Seym vote in 1976 (would the opposition make a showing?), like the day Karol Wojtyla was elected Pope, like the feverish wait for news from the Gdansk shipyards, or a little later, the hours in St. Mary's Church at evening mass during martial law, when Krakow's inhabitants, wrapped in furs and warm jackets, were thinking not of God but of Brezhnev, tanks, and their country.

These were great, unforgettable emotions, sometimes verging on ecstasy. It seemed to me then that I was becoming someone larger than myself alone; that all the border crossings within my individual being had been opened; that all society had become my kin and had entered the depths of my "I"; and as a result I had become stronger, greater, invincible (even if the shared euphoria had been brought on by defeat or political tragedy).

Great, unforgettable emotions—but not entirely mine. When they finally weakened, subsided, I felt a little ashamed. I'd return to my own private life, which always struck me, for a longer or a shorter while, as petty and impoverished, just as any room seems shabbier at the moment when the glaring television spotlights that brighten it go out. I don't have anything against this kind of experience. There's no doubt that such moments have enriched my life, and the lives of other people too. It embarrassed me, though, that they came from without, that I'd done nothing to earn them. I'd borne witness to a gigantic spectacle. But can one make poetry, make art from such emotions?

I'm not siding with the aesthete who insists that history, politics, society aren't proper themes for art. I'm still convinced that everything, including our collective existence (particularly if it is vital and meaningful), can and even must be the subject of the artist's scrutiny. But that touch of shame I felt each time the great emotions faded kept me thinking about the genesis of artistic inspiration; and I grew more and more convinced that a poem, essay, or story must grow from an emotion, an observation, a joy, a sorrow that is my own, and not my nation's. They should arise inside me, and not within the crowd, even if I love the crowd (to love a crowd—good Lord!) and passionately take its part.

The New Wave—and this was both its strength and weakness—drew upon collective emotions, emotions that were at times entirely hypothetical (it's not every day that society deigns to reveal itself in a shipyard or church). A good political cabaret feeds on the thoughts and feelings that an intelligent everyman experiences in a given week or month. The New Wave likewise conducted an ongoing, artistically dangerous dialogue with a putative Critical Citizen, a precursor of the civil society that was just then slowly, painfully being born.

The movement's political merits were not insignificant, even though its poems appeared in editions of eight hundred copies or so. (From today's perspective, even its leftist illusions may have served some purpose. In Poland it may be better to err on the left than on the right; in any case it's more original.) It was a useful and necessary episode in Polish poetry; the aestheticism then seeking shelter beneath the umbrella of the totalitarian censor was rather repellent, and if one understands the New Wave as a reaction against that anomaly, then it's difficult not to rejoice that its poems and manifestos managed to see the light of day.

The New Wave had less attractive features, though. Its didactic fervor, its deep sense of its own righteousness—these were inescapable. And from the political point of view there was in fact no question that right was on the young poets' side. Unfortunately, though, one must distinguish rightness from self-righteousness. Only artistic pedants can safely indulge in displays of their own infallibility.

The New Wave was, by its very nature, a transitional and imperfect artistic phenomenon. It was a compromise between the desire for a truth that would serve the collective citizen and the yearning for a more subtle, fragile truth, the truth of the individual person. It was also a curious compromise between a modern aesthetic consciousness and the acute, seemingly prehistoric pain occasioned by the primitive political oppression to which we were subjected. It was, moreover, a compromise between the will to protest and the paradigm of literary caution that had taken shape in postwar Poland. And on and on—the list of compromises contracted by this uncompromising formation might be continued indefinitely.

How many poems of the New Wave will survive? (Not to mention the artworks by painters associated with the movement.) I don't know. The author maliciously declines to comment. But it's not up to me in any case.

The New Wave was also where I first met the young poets and painters who would become my friends. The young Krynicki, the young Baranczak, the young Kronhold, Kornhauser, Sobocki,

Grzywacz, Karasek, Waltos, Nyczek: the rabid speeches during the Klodzko Spring of Poets, the attacks, the passion, the ridicule, and the faith that someday we'd attain maturity. Urszula Koziol once asked me in Wroclaw if we angry young poets had really made a secret pact to annihilate all our poetic seniors. No, I said truthfully, there was no such pact.

The school of dying: a rather short man arrived in town one day. He was elegantly dressed, although his clothes were at least twenty years behind the reigning fashions.

It was said that he'd conducted dance lessons in the small towns near the foothills of the Carpathian Mountains. He'd apparently gone bankrupt and therefore decided to try his hand at setting up a school of dying.

Many people signed up for his courses, by and large the young, with shining eyes.

Their elders smiled indulgently, thought it over, and by and large declined.

What for, they said, what for. It's common knowledge.

After two months of intensive practice, which inspired extravagant rumors, the master suddenly vanished a few days before the final exam.

One of his disciples committed suicide.

Then vacation started. The summer was exceptionally hot and dry.

Right now, just as my work on this book slowly draws to a close, I'm caught up in Cioran's *Cahiers*, the posthumously published diaries

of the Romanian pessimist; the great skeptic kept his journal from
1957 to 1972. I'd read several of his books earlier, and was taken by
the intensity of his expression. At times, though, his writing seemed
belabored: his despair sometimes read like an exercise in style, and
his point of view was too consistent. It lacked the outbursts of
humor that come naturally to "despairing souls," who never stay in
one place, after all, who run the gamut of complex, contradictory
emotions. What can you say about a "desperate soul" who writes
and rewrites and refines time and again . . . and never casts doubt
on his own doubts? And never bursts out laughing?

The *Cahiers* are different. They contain a vast range of sensa-
tions, from the deepest sorrow to wild rapture; from ecstasies over
Bach to the hit song "Those Were the Days." Cioran lays himself
open in his wandering between the North and South Poles; he
moves from despair to faith, however fleeting. I suddenly encounter
someone close to me, someone I can understand . . . Like the mali-
cious, melancholy Philip Larkin, he can write only when he is
depressed, as he admits in the *Cahiers*; he thus lopped off his spirit's
highest parts. I'm different; I can write only in periods of happiness
or peace.

Do philosophical differences all boil down to this: some people
can write only when they're sad, while others get on better when
they're happy?

The Church of the Franciscans, one of Krakow's countless
churches, stood close by the university. It wasn't especially attractive: fires had destroyed it several times, and it had the misfortune
of being restored in the mid-nineteenth century. Beneath its dreary
neo-Gothic robes, though, it remained one of Krakow's oldest
sanctuaries. I read somewhere that its founder was Prince Boleslaw

the Timid. The same prince who'd intrigued me as a child! It wasn't that I'd studied the historians' accounts of Boleslaw; I'd been struck by his nickname, "the Timid," which led me to imagine all kinds of possible explanations. I liked to think about him, to compare him to the people I knew, to shy friends of my parents, like Mr. Sobertin, who said goodbye while shuffling backward toward the door, to my own shy classmates and professors. I placed him alongside other princes with picturesque nicknames: our Henry the Devout (admirable, but slightly dull, I thought); the angelic John Lackland (this one I liked! I too had lost my land!); the English Richard the Lion Heart; the small but valiant Armspan; Kazimierz the Just; Leszek the Black and Leszek the White (divided like the Dunajec below Zakopane); Boleslaw the Bold (but boldness wasn't and shouldn't be remarkable in a prince). I liked to imagine the bashful prince, blushing beet-red at the slightest provocation. The timid, oxymoronic prince, maybe stammering, avoiding significant political decisions (oh, Machiavelli would not be pleased) and public performances. He'd bequeathed us, nonetheless, a church whose bricks had also grown red many times (in fires).

But the Church of the Franciscans also held Wyspianski's stained-glass window. For a long while stained-glass windows were the least interesting part of any church for me. Perhaps this had something to do with the neo-Gothic church in Gliwice in which I'd done my stint as a not particularly impressive altar boy. This wasn't a case of an ancient shrine shrouded by a banal reconstruction. It was a typical specimen of barracks-style Prussian architecture. Even the churches had a military flavor; their design meant that they could be pressed into the service of local garrisons, exacting sergeants, and love-sick lieutenants. The windows in our church were ugly, drab, and trite, like the drawings of a clumsy child who uses lines and triangles to hide his lack of talent. (I myself was just such a child. I couldn't draw at all and had to resort to tricks in order to deceive my—not overly demanding—teachers.)

In Krakow's old churches, though, you came upon stained-glass windows so dark that you couldn't make out anything but black spots: they'd gone blind. I didn't know the dazzling blue windows of Chartres then; I knew so little about them that I didn't even miss them, I couldn't imagine either them or their mother, the asymmetrical cathedral built of light stone that towered proudly above a small provincial town like the *Iliad* over Greece.

The Zelenski family's stained-glass studio was housed in one of the apartment buildings along Three Poets' Boulevard. A few very elegant homes had small stained-glass windows in their stairwells; they resembled large, colorful butterflies that had alighted on plain, white, ordinary windows. After the last war these gaudy dots gleamed like memories of better, prewar years (ah, my dear, the beef really tasted like beef before the war! And the ham, the ham was pure poetry).

"God the Father—Come Forth!": this was the strange double name, made up of noun and verb, that Wyspianski gave to the overwhelming stained-glass window set in the west wall of the Church of the Franciscans. And it opened my eyes to all that the art of stained glass could be. Installed in 1940, the window was not only nothing like the unintelligible, blackened postage stamps I'd grown up with. It was astonishingly bold, vivid, luminous, aggressive.

Seen from a distance, it seems to depict a blooming tree, a splendid, frenzied African tree that has just reached the intoxicating peak of its beauty. But a strong wind, entirely out of keeping with the peaceful spring day, has taken it unawares. It bends, distraught; it hadn't planned on this hideous wind when it unveiled its beauty.

When we move a few yards closer, God the Father comes into view, an enormous, exotic bird with sumptuous, frayed wings. Like a bird that has just done triumphant battle with a vile serpent: its violet, orange, and red feathers are in disarray but have lost none of their prodigious, tropical intensity.

We come closer still, and the bird becomes a creature of carnival, perhaps a smooth-faced young student dressed up as an old man, who's pasted on a gray beard and placed a thick gray wig upon his head; his garments are marvelously mottled, sewn of rainbow ribbons. Then we perceive that the student disguised as an old man is in the midst of a fiery oration; his left hand seems to repulse a charging mass of impassioned auditors, while his right hand appeases someone else. There is perdition in his gesture too: he damns sin and baseness, and perhaps also the kind of bad art that so enraged Wyspianski.

As we retrace our steps, we're struck above all by the powerful gesture of God the Father (apparently Wyspianski used his father-in-law as the model), who is an exceptional orator along the lines of Piotr Skarga. You will note the figure's motion (certain tour guides speak only in the future tense), and once again, the fin de siècle brilliance of its tattered colors.

But, after all, we have no idea what God the Father looks like (there's certainly no resemblance to Wyspianski's father-in-law); the mutability of Wyspianski's window helps us acknowledge this without inviting agnosticism.

The figure's majestic gesture seems to issue yet another summons: go further, examine other gods, other Fathers, compare them to me, prepare for a long journey. You have to start somewhere. Begin in Paris, view that proud city, shaped by art and the guillotine, marked by the sufferings of the thousands of unknown artists who starved here and by the brief triumphs of those few whose work was recognized sooner or later. Spend many days there, bring good shoes and do a lot of walking. Don't forget la Sainte-Chapelle, lost amid judicial offices. (Surrounded by watchful policemen, overwhelmed with scurrying supplicants and attorneys, la Sainte-Chapelle resembles a provincial maiden speaking her regional peasant dialect, who has brought her wares—stained-glass windows—from her native village to sell, and has been waiting several hundred years for customers. But they all have more pressing business and pay no attention.) Don't forget the Seine's bridges. Stop by the Louvre and the other museums, get acquainted with the paintings of old and new masters, anonymous or known by name. Pay a visit to the "vertical" *Saint Sebastian* (there's also a "horizontal" *Sebastian*, or at least there used to be, now only a copy remains), the *Sebastian* of de La Tour, a painter whose fame came so late; you'll see Saint Irene nursing the wounded youth. Sebastian's smooth young body looks as though it were carved of wood; it rests on the marble floor, while four women's figures rise above him. Saint Irene kneels before the boy with a torch in her right hand (de La Tour requires torchlight to motivate his nocturnal paintings, just as a prose writer needs a narrator and a poet calls for metaphors). And three other women's outlines form above her. Thus the "vertical" *Saint Sebastian* is finally a painting that contrasts healthy, that is, "vertical," humankind with horizontal humanity, failing, powerless, pierced by pain.

Of course, you must get to know the great museums, but don't forget the lesser ones. Drop by the Orangerie and see Soutine's series of paintings, including the bellhop dressed in red who becomes a hummingbird in the midst of the great midnight city. In the same small gallery you'll find Cézanne's portrait of his son. You'll note that the face of the artist's son did not take its shape, as is usually the case, from a dialogue between his parents' genes; it arose instead in conformity with the principles of his father's painting, it is a product of his palette. The boy's cheeks might just as easily have been an apple; Cézanne's son was a still life!

Go for a walk in the rain, in the drizzle of a warm September day—rain's not hard to come by in Paris! Take the side streets and the broad boulevards. In a while, if you're patient and watchful, you'll note with surprise that in this gifted city even damp sidewalks trampled by pedestrians become long strips of canvas, reflecting, as in the atelier of Pissarro or Monet, the sky, the clouds, the rooftops, and the fickle chimneys of old apartment houses. Their shapes will be slightly off-kilter, fanciful, wavy, and wet—but you'll like it, you, who could draw only with triangles and straight lines!

Take a look at the squat little Romanesque churches that conquered the stony hamlets of the Ile-de-France. They're usually closed, but that's all right, it's enough to view them from outside and be moved by their stocky silhouettes. You'll catch the occasional Gothic element: a Romanesque eye set beside a Gothic nose. Don't begrudge the train fare, make the trip from Paris to Chartres. Shiver when you enter the cathedral's mammoth nave, shiver from faith and yearning and even desire, as if this extraordinary temple had awakened us to life, to full life, and not just to routine piety and art understood by the book, as if it spoke, insisted, shouted, that life is whole. While in Chartres, observe the ancient stained glass with its famous azure, dark and opaque at certain points like the fur of mythic animals. You may stroll for a while across the floor's stone slabs; you'll soon understand why so many foreign travelers came to settle in Chartres throughout the ages (some, poor things, earned their keep as guides to the cathedral, trading their otherworldly ecstasy for tips). They couldn't survive without the lifegiving thrill of the cathedral and so stayed on in this provincial town, which had known splendor in the Middle Ages, when theology flourished here, but which had long since been banished to the category of minor municipalities consigned to near oblivion.

Go to Bourges too, visit the cathedral there, and the magical windows in its apse (on cloudy days the stained glass seems to become the windows of a bathyscaphe drifting slowly past a coral reef peopled with submarine prophets and saints). Make your way to Vézelay in Burgundy, but not for the windows this time; observe the rosy stone, the delicate, pink light, and the rhythm of the columns as they make their way like dancers toward the altar. Enter the cathedral in Le Mans and note how the Gothic and the Romanesque, so different, have managed to coexist peacefully within the same building for centuries. Take a trip to southwestern France, which once was part of the medieval kingdom of Catalonia, and visit the Romanesque monasteries, with their cloisters and gardens, their occasionally clumsy, even pre-Romanesque sculpture, people with faces like toads—but even these don't lack a certain round, stony poetry. Stop by the abbey of Saint-Michel de Cuxa up in the Pyrenees, and observe the early sculpture; among these works, you'll even find Hindu deities obediently adorning Catholic cloisters. You'll also see that even Islam could be reconciled with Christianity, at least in stone, and lent its Arabian forms to the Romanesque churches.

And go to Moissac, a little town in the Tarn-et-Garonne department, where you'll find St. Peter's Abbey (it belonged once to the Benedictines). You'll learn that they planned to raze it in the nineteenth century in order to build a railroad! Pause awhile before the twelfth-century statue depicting the prophet Jeremiah. You'll be startled, struck; you'll see the sad, sweet face of the young prophet. You were expecting a stern elder, his face twisted in wrath, but instead you've met the best of creatures, mournful and sensitive, the prophet at rest after a furious diatribe, perhaps alarmed by his own passion.

In southern France you must visit the restored Abbey of Sénanque. The buildings' thick walls were intended to safeguard the concentration of the hardworking, early-rising monks (Cistercians). Before the abbey's walls a field of lavender will bloom, swarming with squadrons of butterflies and bees—and you'll stop short, you'll suddenly catch the same combination of violet and majesty that marks Wyspianski's haughty window.

And if you can't manage such a protracted expedition, if you're too poor, too old, too weak, too lazy, ill, fragile, tired, don't worry, it's not the real trip that counts, the dusty train or crowded highway. It's enough to imagine those noble regions, the noble faces of those paintings and statues, you'll make the journey in your mind and experience a little beauty (since you'll find ugliness, vulgarity, and evil wherever you are, even without my advice). You'll see works of art so finished, so full that they offer more than mere momentary pleasure. They give you something you can keep, something that shapes your very spirit—forms, enchantments that remake reality itself. Come forth, Wyspianski's vivid God the Father tells us, be Boleslaw the Bold, don't be so shy.

I don't know if Ernst Jünger is a great writer, but I do know that he invites us to a great reality.

Imagine the despair of someone who believes in invisible things, in the immortal soul, in human worth, who sees man as a higher being, meant for great deeds, for nobility and fidelity, and who expresses these notions in writing. He lives in cynical times, though, when only what is low receives applause, while higher things are taken as purely rhetorical constructs, as schoolteachers' blather, entirely unmoored from reality. They're met exclusively with scorn and mockery or, most often, with cold indifference. Since this goes on for years, this person comes to the conclusion that he's completely without talent—talent is one of the few higher things to be recognized in the public's eyes—and he falls silent. He's silent, but not forever. Once the quarantine has passed, he begins—timidly at first, but then boldly and loudly—to praise what is low and mock the higher things. (And he does this better than the rest, since, unlike his uncouth rivals, he actually has some knowledge of these things.) His efforts meet with success, he becomes rich and famous. On his deathbed, he begs for forgiveness—it's not clear whose. He's answered by a whisper: Don't worry, it was nothing, that's how it had to be. It had to be; we used you, don't be angry.

To tend the world: read a little, listen to a little music.

Only things of the spirit are truly engaging. But it's nearly impossible to speak of them; they're as transparent as muslin. One can talk only about people and things—talk about them so they'll cast a shadow.

After he lost the French presidential election in 1995, Edouard Balladur apparently studied Epictetus and Seneca (his co-workers would have done well to follow his example): this is the purpose of the Stoics.

Imagine someone who wants to write a defense of poetry. He prepares scrupulously, and spends years on the book. He's three-quarters done when he notices that he's unconsciously begun attacking poetry; he doesn't like it anymore, he sees only its artificiality and pretensions, its bookishness, its inability to answer the most difficult and fundamental questions. But then, as he draws near the end, he forgives poetry once again for its obvious imperfections, and thinks that this is precisely the point: to be able not to answer the most difficult questions, and keep living anyway.

To seek him in solitude, in the bitter leaves of autumn.

God is hidden. Poverty is obvious.

A certain ironic author cites Luther (against himself!): "The Holy Spirit isn't skeptical."

The opposition's countless meetings in the seventies! Discussions, debates—they didn't differ much from other meetings, except that the company was better. The meetings usually took place without event; a police car was almost always parked nearby, but that never ruined anybody's mood. One time in the winter, though, Jacek Wozniakowski and I set off in his hunchbacked Volkswagen for what we considered an extremely important meeting of the Flying University that was being held in Warsaw. There was a lot of snow; the highway had been cleared, but the side streets were drowning in snow. Jacek turned off onto one of these streets, a real cart track. Once we'd finished our breakfast and wanted to get going, it turned out that our car was stuck in a snowdrift. Our efforts were useless, none of our maneuvers helped; the engine wasn't up to it, the wheels spun, but the car stayed put. We were in despair; time was passing, we were going to be late, and we'd been sent by the Krakow division of the Flying University, we had a mission! Fortunately, an athletic-looking peasant appeared on the path after some time. We asked him for help. He rolled up his sleeves and lifted the car up high enough to free it from its snowy bondage. We thanked him profusely, and not without a sense of shame. It took a local athlete to liberate two Krakow insurgents whose goal was to liberate themselves!

My sister's husband, Andrzej, was ill with cancer. He once came to Krakow to see a British faith healer named Harris. He was already very thin, moved only with difficulty, and rarely spoke—he who'd once been the life of the party! I took him to the Church of the Bernardines just beneath the walls of Wawel Castle. The pleasant young student attendants seemed to be from a different world, since they were healthy. They were anxious to see everything go as efficiently as possible (not an easy task, since Harris drew crowds). One had only to glance at the pale, tired invalids who pressed against the altar rail—occupied this time by a healer, not a priest—to understand that the energetic students, young Catholics with open, friendly faces, had nothing in common with these wretched, sickly people who could barely walk.

Andrzej managed to touch Harris's hand, but it didn't do him any good, and he died not long after.

Once we were in Dutch Haarlem one November; when evening fell we went out for a walk. It was already completely dark, and the bountifully lit, curtainless interiors of comfortable apartments brimming with old furniture shone in vivid relief. In one such interior, a young girl was taking an oboe lesson, while her elderly music teacher looked on attentively. Standing on the far side of the glass, we were just shadows, tourists. An oboe lesson in November: it was windless, though the evening was cold. Neither the girl nor her teacher paid the slightest attention to us, the intruders outside the window. For a moment only they existed, absorbed in music.

The misanthrope who says, "I don't want to see people, books are all I need," hasn't yet reached the highest level of initiation. Books are written by people, after all!

I remember how embarrassed I was when—I think it was in 1969—we made our first public appearance as the newly formed poetic movement NOW. It was on a Sunday afternoon in the student club Under the Salamanders, and we read our poetic manifesto. Amazingly enough, the hall was almost full, and held some very intelligent people. And then the gibberish of our program! (There was nothing compromising in the political sense, just plain ordinary nonsense . . .)

Once, near the end of the seventies, I went to see friends who were vacationing in a little seaside town. They were staying at a rest home for priests. Most of the cars parked in front of the building were Russian Moskviches. I asked why there were so many. Didn't you know that the priests all go for Moskviches these days? Not Fiats, not Warburgs, just Moskviches.

Primo Levi and his nightmare: the Polish word *Wstawac*—"Get up"—shouted at dawn in a barracks at Auschwitz. An impersonal word I know from Boy Scout camp (where they were more inclined, in chipper scout fashion, to the phrase "Rise and shine"), and from my brief stint in boot camp. In Gliwice, an adjunct camp of Auschwitz occupied a spot right by the city park, over-looking the dark river; a few modest buildings of dark brown brick remained after the war. These low, empty buildings, overhung more densely every year by alders and other trees, cowered beneath the blows of the wintry drizzle. In summer they stood idle and thoughtless amid the ceaseless activity of clouds and birds. In the park, on the far side of the lazy river, children shrieked at play.

The word *wstawac*, shouted out at dawn by some primitive guard, as the only word of my language!

If only philosophers could learn a single thing from the poets—how not to have opinions!

Every now and then I used to mull over a question to which there was no answer: What would the great, innocent artists of the past,

Giotto or van Eyck, Proust or Apollinaire, have done if some spiteful demon had set them down in our flawed and tawdry world,
warped by so-called totalitarianism? What if they had been plopped
into this world of mindless lies and an omnipresent police force that
was covert and bureaucratic, petty and crude, completely lacking
the imagination of Italy's great Renaissance bandits (which is not to
say that they couldn't ruin people's lives)? Reality expanded in the
hands of the past's great artists, it became enticing and mysterious,
plumed like the wings of a hawk. These artists suffered intensely
from the imperfections of ordinary existence, they had learned to
evade the great flaws that mark every era. How would they have
coped with the vast shadow of our overweening government?
Would they have fallen silent? And what if they had been transported to a wealthy nation, free, but indifferent—what would they
have said?

I first met Adam Michnik in Warsaw in 1973. I had already gotten
to know many intellectuals in the opposition. Almost all of them
spoke sotto voce, not exactly in a whisper, but in carefully modu-
lated tones. Their caution was rational and justified; we all lived
beneath the enormous roof of the secret police, our conscience
had been nationalized, microphones might be hidden in the lamps,
in the flowerpots that held our seemingly innocent plants, in the
walls themselves. We'd all heard stories about bugs concealed in
chandeliers, in tables and sofas. I knew people who kept their
hands over their lips even at home, and who transmitted important information only on scraps of paper, which were then
destroyed. Intellectuals fell into two camps, the conformists and
the resisters, but even these resisted cautiously. Adam didn't
belong to this category. He couldn't be placed in any standard

psychological or sociological bracket. He didn't keep his voice down, he was loud and witty, he radiated courage and joie de vivre. He wasn't a poet, he didn't write poems. But he recited them: he knew scores of poems by heart, Milosz, Herbert, Slonimski. This wasn't the main thing, though; all it takes is a good memory to quote poems. Something else was more important. Adam was then, I think, one of the few happy people in Poland (and perhaps in all of Eastern Europe). I don't mean the kind of private happiness that consists of finding a nice, pretty wife and an interesting, well-paid job, the happiness that comes from the consciousness that you are a healthy, decent, and useful individual. I have in mind the much rarer form of happiness that arises when you locate your true vocation with pinpoint precision, when you find the perfect outlet for your talents, not in the private, domestic sphere, but in the larger human polis.

The mystery of Adam's calling lay in its paradoxical nature. Adam drew upon his own anarchic needs and dreams whenever he confronted—so boldly, with such panache and glee!—the secret police, the Party, corrupt and well-fed prosecutors, dim-witted ministers. He was a joyous anarchist, tossing down his challenge to the vast apparatus of power. He wasn't your typical anarchist, though; he stood for good and honorable things, he sided with right and justice (as they ought to be, not as they were).

A person like Adam who'd happened to live on the other side of the Iron Curtain, in an orderly bourgeois society, would no doubt have turned to dark and evil gods. He would have read and recognized de Sade and the other spiteful, downcast, bitter masters who've turned against the world. He would have praised doubtful powers, made his pact with Satan. In this world, though, Adam realized that he'd been given an extraordinary opportunity. He could be both good and furious at once, both negative and decent, critical and honest, maniacal and just. He could be a subversive, an anarchist, a revolutionary, and, at the same time, a conservative defending basic human decency and order; the order in which we lived had squelched the ordinary, imperfect human world.

I came to know other dissidents later, but only a very few shared Adam's peculiarity, the mad joy he experienced in being an upright anarchist, a reasonable revolutionary who had reconciled fire and water, the passion for destruction and the desire to build. What luck, to find in this world a calling both contradictory and genuine, impossible and actual, that fits one's life like a suit cut by the finest tailor!

One Sunday while I was still a student I returned to Krakow after a short visit to Gliwice. It was a May evening, one of those endless, slowly dimming evenings when all who refuse to leave their cramped apartments lose something irrevocably. I dropped my things off at Dluga Street and set out walking once again. Maybe because I'd just gotten off the train I forgot which city it was for a couple of minutes. The last gleams of the setting sun dotted the sidewalks like bloodstained reflections of ancient Byzantium. Blackbirds called out; their song, which linked the passion of the dark, slow phrase with the total indifference of birds who know nothing, seemed to draw long lines across the sky's glassy expanse. I didn't know anyone, I didn't know which part of the city I was in. I was calm and happy; it wasn't exaltation, simply peace. The houses stood serene and heavy on their lots, accepting light, but no longer reflecting it; their long, old bricks, a dull, deep brown, rested after a full day of doing duty among warm gusts of air. I felt their weight, I felt them pressing the earth. The braids of the stone maiden who adorned one Art Nouveau building had been woven once and for

all; she'd lost her stony comb. The streets were nearly empty, like
the set for a film that will never be made. A laughing group of girls
and boys strolled along the sidewalk, and their laughter held something as endless and provisional as life itself. I watched them with
wild envy. I yearned to be one of them, but at the same time I was
glad I wasn't, since this way I could look at them. I was free, like
them, but by myself, and so I could breathe freely, drawing the
evening's honey-gold air into my lungs. Someone was playing the
piano in one apartment; it was one of Bach's partitas, delicate and
forceful, moving through the twilight with a measured step, like a
lovely woman.

Evening! Such a faulty word. The preparations are long in the
making; there is no sun, only a bright expanse of blue, orphaned,
but not unhappy. It seems as though nothing is happening, nothing
will change, night won't come, but the light wanes slowly, systematically. The city grows ever darker. In a moment the houses go dark,
as though a lamp had been turned out, and with this change they
seem to become more real. The sky, on the other hand, goes on living and pulsating for a long while before the cold stars make their
appearance, and down below, their furry little comrades, the armies
of omnipresent bats, amuse themselves with neurasthenic flights
undertaken in the city's heart, frolicking like cheeky children at
bedtime.

Don Quixote upside down: at one time I thought that my life and the
lives of my close friends looked a little like an inverted version of
Don Quixote. As we know, Cervantes's narrator often tells his story
as if it were a tale of chivalry; this is one of the Spanish epic's chief
constructive principles. Don Quixote has not only devoured such
outdated tales; a good-hearted man, he also embraces their conven-

tions. He ventures forth into the world expecting knightly adventures, hoping to encounter other valiant chevaliers, to save princesses and slay dragons. He expects a lofty world and discovers a base one, vulgar, cruel, and vengeful.

I was as devoted a bookworm as the knight of La Mancha. I'd spent my time in the library, though, absorbed in something radically unlike the Spaniard's chivalrous adventures. I'd pored over all the pessimists, parodists, and skeptics of the last hundred years, admiring their stylistic ingenuity. Thus I was prepared for the worst, so well prepared that I thought at times about never setting foot outside the library (a number of modern writers have tried something similar). I yearned for the safe company of thinkers and poets, where one question alone would engross me, the conflict between poetry and philosophy. Or perhaps the problem of language (those who choose to remain in the library love language above all, more than they love people).

I can't say, though, that when I finally went upon my way I came across only pale, noble knights and fair damsels, instead of the demons, fools, and hangmen I'd been led to expect. But I witnessed and experienced more good than I might have anticipated after reading my gloomy masters. I'd been prepared, by and large, to find myself in a world of darkness, devoid of value, a world in which people not only did not believe in God, but had cast off everything noble and lofty. Or, still worse, they only pretended to believe, and thus further debased the notion of humanity that is our common legacy. Meanwhile, though, I came to know people who managed to combine in some astonishing fashion deep, unostentatious faith with a powerful sense of humor and an unacknowledged love of good that was as active and practical as it was unassuming. I wasn't alone in those old churches; and not all the other visitors belonged to the ranks of careless tourists using their cameras instead of their heads. I found people with whom I could discuss the mysteries, the things that can't be talked about. I encountered many mundane types obediently carrying out the orders of the powers that be (if only the amorphous power of stupidity that typifies mass culture). From time to time, though, I had the great pleasure of meeting wise and self-reliant individuals. I also came across simple people, people who didn't read, who were good in the most essential way. People like the charming old Italian woman who lived in the South of France from whom we used to rent vacation lodgings. She was ill, yet always cheerful and kind; she helped me understand that goodness doesn't come from some theory or principle but from sources deeper than the word.

I didn't witness the extermination of the Jews, I was born too late. I bore witness, though, to the gradual process by which Europe recovered its memory. This memory moved slowly, more like a lazy, lowland river than a mountain stream, but it finally, unambiguously condemned the evil of the Holocaust and the Nazis, and the evil of Soviet civilization as well (though in this it was less successful, as if reluctant to admit that two such monstrosities might simultaneously coexist).

I myself lived in the thick of a lesser totalitarianism, mitigated by the crisis of 1956; here I was not merely a witness and observer but a participant, someone meant to be modified in mind and spirit, a would-be victim. I didn't escape every peril; certain axioms of this perfidious system seemed utterly self-evident to me, at least initially. In the end, though, I emerged whole from this crucible, or nearly whole, and this was largely due to those who saw me through: my parents, the authorities of an older generation, the great poets of my language, intelligent émigré writers, and a handful of courageous contemporaries living in Poland.

Several generations worked together to ensure that, with the passage of time, a system that had seemed so mighty not only could not continue its spiritual invasion but even lost ground; with every year it lost more of its reason for being. Its foundations slowly eroded, grew more unstable every day, until in the end they fell away completely, like a flimsy castle built of matchsticks by some retired mailman or twelve-year-old boy.

Executioners, Goebbels or Molotov, don't write history; that task falls to honest people, who have the final word. In the forties or the late thirties, when false ideals had poisoned almost all of Europe, it would have been hard to believe what has now come to pass: the crimes and lies that had found supporters even among Europe's most enlightened citizens are championed now only by tiny groups of eccentrics and idiots.

Even those intellectuals and artists who began by serving Stalin's civilization underwent a rapid transformation and became its harshest critics. I don't condemn them for their early, youthful intoxication; I'm more inclined to marvel at the generosity of human nature, which offers gifted young people a second chance, the opportunity for a moral comeback. Above all, though, I detect the exceptionally patient and persistent work of goodness, which could not be completely extinguished even in this rather cruel century. Goodness does exist! Not just evil, stupidity, and Satan. Evil has more energy, and can act with the speed of lightning, like a blitzkrieg, whereas goodness likes to dawdle in the most peculiar fashion. This fatal disproportion leads to irreparable losses in many cases. Who can forget that turnabout prompted by the events of 1956, the contemptuously titled "rehabilitation" of the victims of Stalin's terror?

But goodness returns, calm, unhurried, like those phlegmatic, elegantly dressed, pipe-smoking gentlemen detectives in old-fashioned mysteries, who appear upon the scene of the crime the day after it's been committed. It comes back slowly, as if it alone had no access to modern modes of transportation, no train, car, plane, rocket, or even bicycle at its disposal. It returns, though, deliberately as a pilgrim, inevitably as the dawn. Unfortunately, it comes back too slowly, as if it doesn't want to recall that we are tragically caught up in time, we have so little time. Goodness treats us as though we were immortal; it is itself immortal in a certain light, dry way, and it apparently ascribes the same quality to us, dismissing time and the body, our aging, our extinction. Goodness is better than we are.

To the minds of cynics and skeptics the category of the sublime in poetry—indispensable for encounters with the mysteries—is pure hype, or disingenuous at best. You're making it up, there's no such thing, you're trying to make a buck, to get some press . . . Or maybe you're just a snob . . . Then after a while the poet begins to suspect himself of fraudulence for two reasons: first of all, because he himself hears the spiteful charges (which are often made in a witty or at least amusing way); and second, because he too achieves this category only rarely, maybe once in a blue moon. One can even imagine a poet who experiences the sublime and demands a high style to express it, but precisely because this is a rare event that requires patient waiting, in daily life he becomes one of poetry's ironic persecutors. It happens this way because, for unknown reasons, all great things vegetate painfully in our world. Quickly, all too quickly, the sublime turns into suspicion. Returning to its altitudes is even more difficult than the first trip. The laws of gravity are in force even here . . . The category of the sublime is so vulnerable, so fragile—but it is, for all that, our final outpost, thrust to the farthest heights.

———

To wake and fall asleep, drowse off and waken, to pass through seasons of doubt, melancholy dark as lead, indifference, boredom, and then the spells of vitality, clarity, hard and happy work, contentment, gaiety, to remember and forget and recollect again, that an eternal fire burns beside us, a God with an unknown name, whom we will never reach.

CPSIA information can be obtained
at www.ICGtesting.com
Printed in the USA
LVHW091829030120
642456LV00003B/495/P

9 780820 324104